POST-TRAUMATIC GROWTH MINDSET

THE COMPLETE GUIDEBOOK OF TECHNIQUES OF PTSD HEALING AND RECOVERY

A Self-Help Book for Complex PTSD, Anxiety, Depression, and Stress

GLORIA PALMER

CONTENTS

WHY READ THIS BOOK

Congratulations on purchasing *Post-Traumatic Growth Mindset: The Complete Guidebook of Techniques of PTSD Healing and Recovery*. Thank you for choosing this book and making this important investment in yourself. Hopefully, you will find what you are looking for on these pages. As you read this book, you will unlock new coping tools that will allow you to have a new relationship with yourself and your trauma. It will take time to establish post-traumatic growth, but if you are willing to put in the work, you will accomplish it, and you will learn to deal with the issues that could very well cause deterioration in your life if you don't act now. Your trauma is nothing to be ashamed of; instead, it is something that you must look at honestly. Whether your trauma is physical, mental, sexual, or emotional, it doesn't define you, and you can do better.

Do you struggle to feel engaged in your own life because your trauma holds you back? Is doing normal tasks a fight? Is your mental health suffering? Are you looking to not just patch up your trauma but to transform your relationship with yourself and your mental health? Do hopelessness and stress make you wonder if you're a lost cause? If any of these questions relate to you, you likely have trauma that you need to handle with care, and this book will have resources that can teach you how to handle that trauma appropriately.

Remember that you are not alone in this trauma, but you don't have to carry the trauma without doing anything constructive with it.

Millions of people experience trauma in their lifetimes, and no matter what the nature of the trauma, it likely has a deep impact on your well-being and outlook on the world. While trauma is never a pleasant experience, you can take charge of your trauma and get your life back on track. You may not think your trauma is that serious, but if it impacts your ability to do the things you want to do, there's room for improvement. Even small traumas can have a huge impact, so no matter the level of the pain, know that this book can be there for you. Everyone deserves to feel better. Even if you don't have any trauma of your own, this book can be great for people who have loved ones with trauma. By gaining insight into the post-traumatic growth mindset, you can give traumatized loved ones the support and guidance they may need.

This book not only shows you how to get through your trauma, but it teaches you to be better for it. Pain can lead to great things if you know how to channel that pain and let it guide your personal development.

So many books highlight the importance of this subject. I appreciate that you have selected this one to help you learn about post-traumatic growth. It was also crafted to ensure that it's easy to understand for anyone who wishes to read it. Please enjoy! It's time to change your life for the better and confront your trauma. Don't delay; start creating the change that you want and deserve. If you are suffering, you need to take the time to invest in yourself. Give yourself the gift of healing and self-improvement. That gift will allow you to change your life in so many ways, many of them not directly related to your trauma. When you start to deal with your trauma, you'll have new time and energy to focus on the things that make you the most passionate because it is through those passions that you find joy in life!

INTRODUCTION

P TSD and trauma are all too prevalent in society, and they cause immense emotional distress for the people who experience them. Often, such mental conditions are stigmatized, which can make it even more difficult for people to seek the help they need to get better. According to the National Center for PTSD, around seven to eight percent of adults in the United States will have PTSD in their lifetimes, and eight million will have PTSD at any given time, but the rates of trauma are even higher. Around sixty percent of men and fifty percent of women will experience trauma. Thus, trauma is not something that should be taken lightly, especially when that trauma causes conditions like anxiety, stress, depression, and PTSD.

This book will begin by discussing what trauma is and the symptoms that are common when you have trauma. There are various types and levels of trauma, and when you have a more nuanced view of trauma, you can start to understand your own trauma better. Further, this book will describe how trauma can result in PTSD, but it's important to understand that while trauma and PTSD have an overlap that they are not the same as one another. Further, complex PTSD comes with additional challenges and tendencies that you need to keep in mind as you start to learn the PTSD healing mindset. The more you know about the inner workings of trauma and PTSD, the easier it is to combat the challenges and utilize the processes of your body to promote healing.

The book will also explain the brain-body connection of PTSD, which will enrich your understanding of how PTSD works and how to combat it. Many people think that conditions are just physical or just mental, but trauma manifests in both physical and mental ways, and the connection between your mind and your body can worsen or improve your trauma depending on how you use that connection. This connection is vital because the body's natural response and mental processes are inherently connected. By understanding this connection, you can start to shift your reactions so that you respond in ways that are more healthy. Neurobiology may seem complicated and scary to people who aren't familiar with its concepts, but this book will teach it in a way that you can easily understand, no matter what previous knowledge you have about neurobiology.

Another important lesson you will learn in this book is various coping styles and how these coping styles can either be healthy or unhealthy. Many people rely on unhealthy coping styles, but when you learn to transform your coping style to something that is healthier, your outlook on life and the way you live your life will change. If you're not aware of your coping style, you will be by the end of this book, and you may learn new things about yourself that you have never even considered before.

Crucially, this book will teach you everything you need to know about post-traumatic growth and how to apply it to your life. The most important part of this process is finding tools that you can use to lessen the impact of your PTSD or trauma. Both formal therapeutic methods and less formal methods can be transformative when you get in the habit of using them on a daily basis. Journaling, improved interpersonal relationships, therapy, and connection with animals are just some of the techniques that this book will detail, and while they seem like insignificant steps, they can make a profound impact. There's a wide range of steps you can take, and these steps may feel overwhelming at first, but starting with some of the more manageable steps in this book can ease you into the process. You can then build up to techniques that may be harder for you as you start this journey.

You will learn both physical and mental techniques for healing your trauma. Because of the connection your mind and body have, it's vital that you use both types of techniques that meditate the mental and physical processes that can make it hard to deal with trauma and PTSD. The approach in this book is multifaceted, so it relies on you applying multiple methods, which will lead to holistic healing. There's never just one cure to complex problems like trauma, and the solution is not one size fits all, which is why this book outlines the options you have and enables you to choose what works for you and set aside what doesn't. While some techniques have been found to work based on research, people are unique and have different types of trauma. Thus, suggesting a one-size-fits-all plan would be negligent. By using both physical and mental techniques, you can create a process that is customized to you.

There will be a specific section in this book that details several therapeutic models. With so many types of therapy around, it's often hard for people to know what to look for and what treatment options will be best for them. If you use this book properly, it can help you better learn crucial details about the treatments available, and it will answer some of the questions and uncertainties that may prevent you from starting or continuing therapy. While therapy can be highly helpful, if you don't make the right therapeutic choices for your needs, it might not help you, and it can discourage you from therapy altogether.

Finally, the book will outline how to manage your expectations and continue your work on post-traumatic growth. You cannot expect this project to be magic, nor can you expect that it will happen overnight. You will have lots of changes as you experience post-traumatic growth, and when you manage your expectations, you can monitor these challenges and stay hopeful about your progress. The progress may seem slow, and it may be hard for you to see at first, but if you look back on your journey, you'll be able to see how much progress you've made by applying the techniques herein. These lessons are invaluable for anyone who feels stuck in a trauma spiral. Without further ado, it's time to learn the post-traumatic growth method.

CHAPTER 1

UNDERSTANDING TRAUMA

I t is very likely that if you are reading this book, you have experienced some sort of trauma in your life. Trauma is widely experienced by people, and most people will have trauma at some point in their lives. The hard fact is that anyone can be traumatized. It doesn't matter who you are because it can creep into your life. Around the world, people from all places and demographics deal with trauma, and almost seventy million people experience trauma globally, and those numbers could be on the rise. Based on the predicted United States population, the people who have one traumatic event usually go on to have multiple traumatic events throughout their lifespan. While no precise number exists, several studies performed in the United States have shown lifetime exposure to any kind of trauma to be between 39.1% and 89.6%. On a worldwide level, an estimated 70.4% of respondents experienced lifetime traumas. And that was before the onset of the COVID-19 pandemic of 2020, which researchers are warning could create a global impact on people's mental health. The pandemic is highly traumatic for many people, and that mass trauma is profound.

Accordingly, it is even more important to understand trauma and its role in human lives.

But what is trauma? You've probably heard the word millions of times, but you may not know what separates trauma from normal pain, annoyance, or discomfort. Trauma is so hard to define because it evokes such a wide range of feelings and responses. It is not the same for anyone who experiences it. As a result, creating a concise definition is difficult, leading to an unclear definition among the public.

The word trauma is thrown around so often that its meaning can become diluted. Trauma can become the object of jokes, but it is no joking matter. Psychological trauma especially has developed into a very popular concept in common language and mass media. Some might say it has become a term that has been so casually thrown about that it has become devoid of its true meaning. It's very likely that you or someone you know have used the expression "I was traumatized by it" or "It was a traumatic experience" without giving much thought to the word.

For people who have trauma, while joking about it can help them cope, trauma is profound, and it can influence the way they live their lives and interact with the world. It's not a word that you can apply anytime you feel discomfort or pain. Though, that's not to say that seemingly "little" events cannot lead to a person being traumatized. Trauma matters because it has both physical and mental impacts on ordinary people globally, and it doesn't differentiate based on race, gender, or religion. While some groups may be more at risk—often due to societal and genetic factors—anyone can be traumatized, so the next time you use the word trauma, you may want to consider the full meaning of the word. It's time to unpack the meaning of trauma

The terms "stress," "crisis," "trauma," along with other similar words, are often treated as synonyms. When you experience each of these things, you may have similar feelings and experiences, but they all have nuances that make them stand out. In many ways, they exist on a continuum. Each affects people on an individual level, but it is imperative to note the similarities and differences between these terms. Let's try and draw some distinctions between them. Remember that you can experience these things all at once, and these things can increase your odds of the others (if you are more stressed, an event is more likely to become traumatic, for example, because you are already vulnerable).

Stress

Stress is unavoidable and perfectly normal. We all will feel it during our lifetime. When you have a demand on your body or your mind, you have stress. The stress statistics show how much this concept is part of daily life for people. Virtually all people experience stress regularly, and this stress is commonly related to things like work, interpersonal issues, and health concerns. The American Psychological Association (APA) says that thirty-three percent of Americans experience extreme stress. Further, among all people in America, seventy-seven percent will suffer from the physical side effects of stress, such as fatigue, headaches, or tense muscles. Stress not only can cause health problems like increased blood pressure, but it can also cause worsened mental health, so it can cause anxiety, depression and make a person less resilient to traumatic events.

Evidently, stress is not only widespread, but it impacts people severely because it causes both physical and mental symptoms.

Most research focuses on bad stress, but stress isn't all bad, though. While people mostly focus on the stress that makes their lives difficult, it also helps to understand how stress can be beneficial. If you think about the times you are stressed, some trends may become evident. Stress isn't always an awful feeling, though. Sometimes, it is good, and it encourages you to do better and to rise to the occasion. Unfortunately, it can also make it hard for you to focus, and you might find yourself unable to concentrate and prone to procrastination because of maladaptive stress. Bad stress can cause negative health outcomes, so it can be debilitating for people who experience it.

Good stress is commonly referred to in the psychological community as "eustress." This kind of stress is what you have when you feel enthusiastic. You'll probably feel your hormones start to flow, and your pulse will quicken. You are not afraid, and you don't feel as though you are in danger. It is like riding an intense amusement park ride or when you are vying for a promotion or going on a date with someone you haven't met before. When you are getting married, having a baby, or experiencing other life changes, you may feel stress, but this stress stems from a sense of excitement. The unknowns cause your body to respond, but it also marks having stimulation and change that humans often need to feel fulfillment. When you're working on an intense work project, you may feel your heart racing as you try to finish it, but this feeling isn't necessarily that dreadful all-consuming stress. And instead, it propels you toward the finish line. So many things can evoke this stress, and these things keep you motivated, and they give you things to keep you going when things get hard in life.

The type of stress that you may commonly think of when you hear the word stress is acute stress, and this stress is more alarming. This stress is your body's fight or flight reaction, which means that it is the sense of panic you feel when your brain decides that it could be in danger, and you must quickly decide whether you want to fight or flight. When something surprises you, you have this stress because unexpected things are interpreted by your brain as dangerous. Acute stress causes a stress response that is markedly unpleasant. This stress is what we normally think of as "stress" (or "bad stress"). This stress isn't inherently bad, even if it makes you feel bad. It is your body's natural response to threatening stimuli. Your body has this automatic response because it has evolved to realize that a conscious decision-making process can be too slow. Thus, when your body senses danger, it turns to automatic processes meant to safeguard you. If you're in nature and you come across a bear, for example, going through all the options and analyzing the situation would be too slow, but by having a fight or flight reaction in place, you use your instincts to make quick decisions. This reaction has drawbacks, and in the modern world, you can have this reaction at inappropriate times, but it's meant to help you survive dangerous situations.

You can remedy the hardship of acute stress by learning relaxation techniques and employing them when you feel the onset of this stress. After you have handled the stressor, it takes time to put your body back in balance and get your mindset to its pre-stress calmness. When you have this stress, you'll feel your body start to react. Your heart may quicken, your hands may shake or stress, and your thought process may shift. We've all felt that moment of panic when the acute stress kicks in, and after, it can take a little while to recover. Nevertheless, breathing methods and relaxation can help you get your bearings back speedily.

Another type of stress is chronic stress, and this stress is the kind of stress that can wear you down. You get this type of stress when you have inescapable stressors that repeat and never seem to relent. This stress becomes all-consuming. It may come from a high-stress job or a tense family situation, among other things. When you have this stress, it is *serious stress*. Your body isn't meant to endure stress in such a prolonged manner, so when you have this stress, it's going to have a huge impact on your well-being. Unfortunately, this type of stress is the type that people normally try to ignore. They try to push past it rather than working through it.

When you have fleeting and constrained stress, stress can help you. It encourages you to complete challenges, and it motivates you when you're working on projects. You can become more efficient with good stress. Stress has been shown, in some cases, to even increase your memory! Stress is often a driving force in your life, which is why you shouldn't discount it altogether. At the very least, stress gives you information about your state of mind and is a great gauge for your emotional and physical needs.

Stress also keeps you alert to dangers, and it produces the fight-or-flight response, which we've already touched on. Your body experiences a flood of chemical responses when you are under stress, and these chemical reactions cause your body's physical and emotional responses that are so characteristic of stress. You may start to have higher blood pressure and a speedy heart rate, for example. Stress keeps you safe because it helps you become more aware of what's happening around you in many instances of danger, and you'll learn how this response can also have negative results. In any case, stress is not always a bad thing until it becomes a chronic issue and disallows you to ever relax properly.

But before we detail the negative, maladaptive side of stress, let's detail the health impacts of having healthy levels of stress. Several studies have shown that stress can benefit your immune system, which means that you get sick less likely and may have a lower likelihood of autoimmune disorders! Further, stress can negatively influence your heart health when you have high levels of stress, but as is always the case, moderate levels of stress can actually improve your heart's functioning. One prominent study highlights that people who had some stress prior to surgery had a better recovery prognosis, meaning that they recovered faster. With all these health benefits, stress seems pretty useful, but too much stress and chronic stress often have an adverse effect.

Chronic stress is going to lead to both mental and physical symptoms. One of the most substantial impacts of chronic stress is heart issues. Stress is linked to increased blood pressure, which is a factor that can then influence your heart health and the development of heart disease, which is the number one killer among adults in the United States. Beyond just your blood pressure, chronic stress influences the chemical balance of your heart, which can lead to heart disease and impact your arteries' functioning. Your immune system can suffer from this stress. You may sleep less and feel more aches and exhaustion. This stress can lead to mental health issues like depression, anxiety, and substance abuse.

Stress is never anything that you should feel shame about because it is so typical for people to have. We all will experience it in our lives. The things that stress us out will be different, but there are common threads that connect our stress. Relationships, work, family issues, trauma, injury, and illness are just some of the factors that can cause bad stress, but nearly anything that is difficult for you can do so. Positive stress comes from exciting events like the birth of a new child in the family or a marriage. Understanding the differences between the types of stress that you feel can help you reorient your mindset and your relationship with stress.

You can know that your stress is a problem when you feel overwhelmed, and you turn to coping methods that promote self-destruction and stagnancy rather than growth. Acute stress is often caused by one event, such as a broken bone, while chronic stress can be caused by ongoing events or a series of events. For example, you may get fired from your job and then experience a painful accident, and those events create a situation that gives you enduring stress. Stress often leads to more stress. When you've already got a lot on your mind, smaller things may add to your stress more than they normally would. When you have stress, you may be prone to additional stress. Accordingly, little stressors can start to bother you when they wouldn't normally. This build-up is often unhealthy, and it results from ignoring your chronic stress. Chronic stress can help you lose sight of the joys related to stress (the stress of planning a wedding, for example, may reduce the positive stress that comes with getting married!)

You may struggle to know what kind of stress you are dealing with because you may have multiple types of stress at once, which causes your feelings about each stressor to muddle. Listen to the signs your body is giving you to get a better idea of how you're dealing with your stress.

It may be tough to tell when you're experiencing good or bad stress, but there are important ways that your body lets you know that you're struggling with too much stress. Watch out for the following warning signs:

➢ You may struggle to focus

➢ You may notice that you are getting ill more often

➢ Tiredness and generalized aches are common

➢ You may experience flare-ups of issues you already have

➢ Headaches

➢ Moodiness and irritability are common side-effects of stress

➢ Sleep issues also indicate stress

➢ You may eat too much or too little

➢ People with too much stress often are overly angry or anxious

It's true that stress is unavoidable, but our reactions to it are very individual. How your best friend responds to stress versus how you respond to stress will probably look incredibly different. Your stress reaction is usually determined by a combination of factors like your past experiences, your genes, your personality, and what kind of people you have in your life. The type of stressor and the severity of it will also help dictate your response. Things that are highly stressful for one person may not be stressful at all for another person. Thus, there is little point in comparing your stress to that of other people because what's healthy for you may not be healthy for other people. What stresses you unhealthily may be a healthy kind of stress for other people, so evaluate your reactions and use those reactions to your advantage going forward.

Crisis

In the psychological realm, a crisis is not defined as a traumatic occasion. Instead, it refers to the way that people respond to the reactions. A crisis is defined, therefore, by what happens after. There's a good reason for that; as we've discussed, what is healthy for one person, isn't healthy for other people. Accordingly, what one person calls a crisis won't be a crisis for another person. In Chinese, the word crisis combines the words "danger" and "opportunity." Meanwhile, in Greek, the word crisis is not good or bad, and it suggests an occasion that requires a decision, a turning point of sorts. Thus, a crisis marks a moment that may be hard, but it is not lasting. It is a time that brings change, but it will not last forever.

It's part of being human to have these moments of crisis. At its most severe, a crisis can be an unstable situation of extreme danger or difficulty. During a time of significant crisis, one is likely to feel caught in a downward spiral of poor or challenging coping and possibly maladaptive behavior (i.e., avoidance, withdrawal, substance abuse, anger, etc.). However, after the crises abate, the individual will most likely return to their usual level of pre-crisis level functioning.

When you are in a crisis, you go from "equilibrium to disequilibrium and back again" (Golan, 1978). Simply put, a crisis is an event that rocks your world enough so that you have a hard time functioning, but ultimately, you regain your footing and can go on with life. A crisis can be broken down into five parts.

1. **The Hazardous Event:** When you have a hazardous event, it throws your life out of balance. This event can be something that you know is coming, but it may also be something that you aren't prepared to experience. This event creates the reaction that follows and can cause a spiral. It builds urgency.

2. **The Vulnerable State:** A hazardous event is deemed as hazardous based on your interpretation of that event. Thus, you start to feel dread and worry about what is to come after the hazardous event. You then are in a vulnerable state, and you begin to feel tenser. You try to reduce the tension you feel with coping strategies. These strategies may be unhealthy. If you cannot cope, you start to lose your ability to function.

3. **The Precipitating Factor:** The precipitating factor is the thing that determines whether you will continue from your vulnerable state into a state of crisis. You can view this as the "last straw." It is the thing that sends you over the edge into crisis. It can be a wide

4. **Active Crisis State:** The active crisis state marks a time when you do not have the balance you need to feel safe, secure, and happy. You may experience sleep or eating issues. You may also struggle to focus and become obsessed with whatever event happened. You may also have emotional issues like depression or anxiety. During this stage, you often want to get help because of how distressed you are.

5. **Reintegration:** The final stage is reintegration, and in this stage, you can get your life back into balance.

For the purposes of this book, we'll view a crisis as the reaction you have to stressful events that make it hard to live your normal life (Roberts, 2000: 516). When you are in a psychological crisis, you have a stressful event that you don't know how to remedy with typical coping mechanisms, which then makes it hard to deal with the stressful event.

Some crises are obvious, such as getting fired or divorcing your spouse, but they can also be more complicated. The main factors of crisis are how you respond to an event and how you attempt to resolve that event. Without those factors, you cannot define a crisis as something distinct from a normal event.

People react to crises in a range of ways, and they often rely on techniques that they learned as kids or whatever is quick, easy, and available. It's common for people to use healthy coping mechanisms, such as talking to a support system and working through the crisis in a constructive manner. This group of people will learn to grow from the crisis and be better for it. There is another group that will not deal with what has happened, and they will push the event from their memory—this type of coping increases their chances of having future crises. The unresolved issues will continue to trouble this group of people. The third group of people is those who do not know how to cope without professional help from mental health professionals. They may struggle to be resilient and lack confidence in their ability to escape the crisis.

Again, how we respond to a crisis can vary from event to event, and while you may tend to respond to a crisis in certain ways, based on the exact circumstances of the situation, the response is always going to vary, and accepting that your response is normal and valid can help you deal with the crisis more swiftly and with less judgment.

Trauma

In Greek, trauma is the word for "wound," and this is an accurate depiction of what trauma is. The Greeks reserved the use of this word for people who had physical trauma, but since the creation of the word, it has been expanded to emotional hardships as well (Echterling et al., 2005). According to the American Counseling Association, trauma can be distinguished into two categories – physical, which encompasses bodily injury that cannot be healed without medical attention; and psychological and emotional trauma that affects an individual's "spirit, and sometimes the will to live, as well as beliefs about the world and oneself, dignity, sense of security, thinking, and feeling" (Fact Sheet #7).

Some other definitions of trauma are as follows:

Based on information from the Substance Abuse and Mental Health Services Administration (SAMHSA), trauma can be understood as follows: "Individual trauma results from an event, series of events, or set of circumstances that is experienced by an individual as physically or emotionally harmful or life-threatening and that has lasting adverse effects on the individual's functioning and mental, physical, social, emotional, or spiritual well-being." (SAMHSA, 2014, p. 7). This description shows the expansiveness of traumatic experiences in a concise but inclusive way. Trauma, in general, is a sense of danger, and it doesn't matter if the trauma actually threatens your life; if your life or well-being feels threatened, you can have resulting trauma.

According to the American Psychological Association, trauma is an intense emotional response to an event like an accident, witnessing or being subject to physical or sexual assault, or living through a natural disaster like an earthquake. This definition leaves even more room for interpretation and leaves the definition of trauma open to the individual experiences and feelings that people have. This definition highlights how trauma often is based on how people feel rather than what has happened to them. While what happens to a person can influence trauma, two people can experience the same events, and one may consider it a trauma while another may not. Part of what makes trauma is the traumatizing event or events, but a larger part is the way you process those events.

When you have trauma, your world starts to change, and the way that you look at everyday activities shifts with the traumatized mindset. People who have trauma have extra fear, and they may feel like they are no longer in control of their feelings and life. Often, your trauma relates to other traumas or hardships that you have experienced, so to understand your current trauma, you have to look at present fears and how those fears may relate to your mindset.

When you have trauma, you have trauma on a continuum, which means that not all trauma will be as painful as other trauma, and some will be more enduring than others. Of course, that doesn't mean that trauma is ever invalidated, but it means that how you experience trauma will differ from experience to experience, and you should never feel like your trauma isn't bad enough to matter or think that it may be too bad to treat. Harder trauma may take longer for you to recover from, but that doesn't mean it is insurmountable. Similarly, trauma doesn't have to be that hard to get over, and you shouldn't feel guilty or like there's something wrong with you if you bounce back easily. For example, when someone loses a family member, they might take months to recover, while another person may only take a few weeks. Hurts heal at various rates, and that's okay.

Everyone has different sensitivities, so when dealing with your trauma and other people's trauma, don't use judgment. Be more understanding and realize that being merciful with yourself is a great way to improve your journey. Be content with where you are on the continuum. Let yourself recover from trauma at the rate that best suits your needs and the nature of your trauma. When you learn to do that, you can learn to grow even with your trauma, but you can also be ready for future trauma that may be less severe or more severe!

Psychological trauma is one of the most difficult types of trauma to treat because it isn't as concrete as physical trauma. It is often hard to understand. While you see physical trauma, this trauma can exist under the surface, which makes it easier to push away and ignore than a physical injury. Nevertheless, it festers, and it can cause serious danger when you don't tend to this trauma. Physical trauma can also cause psychological trauma. For example, if someone has a serious bodily injury that makes them less mobile in some way, they may also have emotional responses to that same trauma.

The following are potential (but not an exhaustive) list of causes of trauma:

> Bullying
> Natural disasters
> Chronic physical illness and terminal illnesses

- ➢ Any kind of abuse or sexual trauma
- ➢ Car and vehicle accidents
- ➢ Giving birth to a child
- ➢ Harassment
- ➢ Grief caused by the loss of a person or thing
- ➢ Violence or being the victim of a crime
- ➢ Terrorist acts and military conflicts

Approximately 80% of individuals that go through a traumatic life event, after a period of stress, readjust and bounce back to previous levels of functioning. This ability to bounce back into a state of equilibrium is commonly known as resilience (Jackson-Cherry & Erford, 2014). Resilience is so important because it allows people to deal with trauma and continue to thrive even after bad things have happened to them. Persons who, for various reasons, are unable to function normally can experience the long-term effects of trauma. Thus, the trauma can continue to impact their lives, and traumatic responses can actually lead to additional trauma.

Types of Trauma

Not all trauma is the same. As such, the type of trauma a person experiences will impact how they respond to and/or cope with that trauma. Knowing the types of trauma can help you understand how trauma can be onset. The various kinds of trauma include:

Acute trauma: This trauma is caused by exposure to a single overwhelming event/experience. Some people may eventually develop acute stress disorder (ASD), which is also known as the acute stress reaction. Acute trauma, like acute stress, comes on quickly and after just one event. Examples of such events include:

- Natural disasters, including hurricanes, earthquakes, wildfires, and floods
- Vehicle accidents
- Incidents of assault, physical or sexual
- Grief
- Medical diagnoses

When you have ASD, you may have intrusive memories. It is also common to have flashbacks and nightmares. People with ASD may struggle to sleep properly and have increases anxiety. It may be hard to focus, and a person's anxiety may become more intense. Further, you may be moody and try to avoid the memories that you're having about the event. You may also have physical symptoms. For example, you may have an increased heart rate and struggle to take a deep enough breath. You may also feel sick to your stomach and jittery.

Acute trauma usually occurs shortly after the traumatic incident, and it can go away pretty quickly, but the symptoms may last for several weeks as your body starts to get back into balance after the trauma. Women more than men tend to develop ASD, but anyone can experience it, and the development of this condition relies on many of the factors discussed throughout this book.

People who have ASD do not always get PTSD, but having ASD may increase your chances of eventually having PTSD. When you learn to manage your ASD, you reduce your chance of developing PTSD.

Complex Trauma: When a person has complex trauma, they have traumatic events that reoccur. They occur within an extended timeframe. Complex trauma was first described as a way to better understand the lasting impacts of child abuse (Herman,1992). Since the initial use of this term, it has come to include other cases of domestic violence and trauma related to attachment. Thus, this type of trauma relates to familial relationships as well as other intimate relationships. It also includes other ongoing trauma that may be outside the domestic sphere. For example, refugees, people who have experienced war or conflict, and human trafficking are some instances that can lead to complex trauma. Complex trauma may also stem from people who have chronic illnesses that are usually painful and may require extensive medical treatment and can hinder everyday behavior.

People who experience this type of trauma generally feel the same type of symptoms as people with ASD, but they also have some other symptoms that may be added to the usual emotions and physical responses.

➢ Suicidal thoughts or behaviors

➢ Self-mutilation like cutting, burning, or hitting oneself

➢ Seeking revenge

➢ Giving more power to the perpetrator

➢ Guilt or shame about what happened

➢ Feelings of despair, hopelessness, or helplessness

➢ Substance abuse issues

➢ Dissociative episodes

➢ Feelings of alienation or self-isolation

> ➢ Struggling with one's concept of self
> ➢ Being unable to trust other people
> ➢ Attachment issues

Complex trauma may be harder to understand, and the sources of this trauma may be multifaceted. Thus, it can be harder to untangle the causes and the incidents that cause this type of trauma. If you have this trauma, you may not even understand the extent of your trauma and the complexities that feed into this trauma. As a result, when dealing with this trauma, it's vital to be patient as you confront your issues and try to determine how that trauma impacts you.

Developmental trauma: When someone experiences trauma that spans during development stages— infant, child, youth— they may have developmental trauma. This type of abuse can come from being abused sexually, physically, or emotionally. It can also occur from neglect. Children who have witnessed violence are more prone to this trauma. Additionally, the death of someone close to them can be traumatic. This trauma interferes with the natural development of the child, and it may make it harder for children to form healthy attachments both in childhood and adulthood. This type of trauma puts people at a huge risk for developing PTSD.

How Early Childhood Trauma Stands Out

When young people experience trauma, they may be confused and struggle more than an adult would to healthily process trauma, especially when the trauma may stem from the fact that they don't have an adequate system of caregiving, and they may be unable to trust the people in their lives who would ordinarily be a support system for them.

Traumatic events have a profound impact on young people, and unfortunately, young children are often especially helpless when confronted with hardship. This helplessness can prolong trauma and make it hard for the child to understand their feelings and situations. Additionally, they may be stuck in traumatic situations that only further their negative symptoms. Stimuli may make children feel unsafe and scared when those stimuli remind the child of hardships they have endured. They may hate loud noises or quick motions, for example. Children often experience nightmares and vivid images related to their trauma, and this trauma is so hard to combat because children are especially vulnerable. Being vulnerable to trauma and less able to process that trauma on their own, childhood trauma is unique, and it can have long-term ramifications for people; thus, this trauma often feeds into adult trauma.

Children are naturally self-orientated. They cannot understand that when something happens to them that it does not reflect on who they are as a person. Thus, trauma can confuse a child. For example, a child who experiences abuse may attribute that abuse to a negative quality in themselves, even though the abuse was not their fault. A child cannot conceive that bad events would happen to them without the child having done something bad. Thus, they often attribute bad things that have happened to them as something that is their fault. Children tend to think that bad things happen because they are somehow bad, which can make events even more hurtful for youngsters.

Children are not old enough to care for themselves, and they rely on adults in their lives to do so. Their worlds are centered around themselves, and they interpret events differently based on their developmental stage. A five-year-old will interpret something in a different way than a ten-year-old would. In any case, they try to make traumatic events make sense, and they try to figure out how they acted that caused the negative experiences. They think that if they can adjust their behaviors and "be a better child," that they can avoid future pain. They don't understand that not everything has a reason, and when a man hits his wife in front of his children, for example, it is not a reflection of the child's behaviors. Some things are just beyond the child's control.

When children deal with trauma, they are at extra risk because this trauma can change the structure of the brain because it happens during developmental years. The cortex of the child's brain may be smaller when they have trauma, and so functions like perception, memory, and the processing of conscious thoughts may be hindered. Young children are vulnerable on a number of levels. As a result, trauma can make the child feel perpetually in danger, especially when it is complex trauma. The child may begin to overgeneralize and assume things about the entire world based on very limited knowledge of what the world is like, and that knowledge is often limited to their familial situations or relationships with other caregivers.

Children who endure trauma because of caregivers' inattention or abuse often have relationship insecurity that follows them into relationships, which means that fulfilling relationships may feel dangerous, and they may expect the worst in people. Children often form their perception of all relationships based on the relationship they had with caregivers in their formative years. The child needs to be able to express their feelings and learn to control their emotional responses, especially when they experience trauma, and without a supportive environment, the trauma will linger, and it will follow the child into adulthood. That trauma will become engrained in their mindset, and it can take a lot of work for an adult to bring that old trauma to the surface and make sense of it. Thus, parents need to be vigilant when their child has undergone trauma, but in some cases, the parent will worsen or even cause that trauma, which is yet another example of why childhood trauma can be so complex and hard to manage.

When children undergo trauma, they can have a number of responses, and noticing behavioral shifts is a major indicator that something is going on with the child. They can experience many of the symptoms of adults, but they may also experience symptoms of their own, like crying more or not wanting to leave their caregivers. Children may experience other mental health issues like anxiety, depression, or mood changes. They may throw tantrums and not know how to deal with their emotions. Some children regress and are no longer able to do things for themselves that they did before. They may struggle in school. Nightmares and flashbacks are also common. Older kids may turn to impulsive behaviors like self-harm, substance abuse, or reckless sexual behaviors.

Children, no matter how young or old, can be impacted by trauma, and because they are in their formative years, that trauma can impact them in complex ways that reflect where they are in their development. Each child will respond to their trauma in unique ways, reflecting their experiences and conditions.

Post Traumatic Stress Disorder

While trauma doesn't always lead to a diagnosable disorder, it can lead to a series of concerning symptoms that don't seem to go away. When the impacts of trauma are prolonged and amplified, it can become post-traumatic stress disorder. Post-traumatic stress disorder (PTSD) is a mental health disorder that is induced by a traumatic event, which a person can either witness or experience directly. People with PTSD may have anxiety, nightmares, and flashbacks related to the traumatic events they have experienced. They have heightened responses to perceived danger.

In its history, people have called PTSD by many names like "shell shock," which they used for traumatized men of WW1. They used the term "combat fatigue" for sufferers post-WWII. PTSD is now known to be something that happens to more than people who have been to war. No matter who you are, you can develop PTSD. According to the National Center for PTSD, up to eight percent of people will experience PTSD at some point in their lives. While there's no exact formula for PTSD, several predispositions will increase the likelihood that someone will have PTSD. Previous trauma, gender, and age are all some things that may impact whether someone will develop PTSD, Though, to reiterate, there's no certain equation that can tell you whether a person will develop PTSD from their trauma.

Most commonly, PTSD symptoms begin right after the trauma has happened, but they might take months or years to appear. The symptoms may also change over time, so the disorder might not even look the same within an individual. These variances can make it hard to recognize that something is wrong or to get help for their condition. When the side effects endure more than four weeks, there is a likelihood you might have PTSD.

CHAPTER 2

WHAT IS PTSD?

Common PTSD Myths

In the last chapter, you learned a basic overview of PTSD, but there is so much more to it, and to understand what it is and its extensiveness, PTSD requires a whole chapter of its own. PTSD is commonly known, and research continues to develop on this topic, but that doesn't mean that people understand it as well as they could. PTSD is so much more than the "shell shocked" veterans that it initially described. Our understanding of this condition has immensely evolved since it was first recognized, but there are still many misconceptions that fuel the discussions around this diagnosis. The stigma created makes it harder for people to access help and accept that they have a problem. Thus, part of dealing with PTSD is learning more about it and pushing through some of the misconceptions.

The Symptoms of PTSD Occur Only Right After the Traumatic Occasion

PTSD doesn't always start right after a traumatic event. While in many cases, symptoms do start right away, there is actually a delayed onset of PTSD, so symptoms can develop months or years after the event has occurred. Only four to six percent of people with PTSD have a delayed onset, but it does happen, so this type of PTSD should never be discounted, and no matter how long it has been since the traumatic event, if you feel these symptoms, you should consider seeing a professional and discussing your concerns. Often, this type of PTSD occurs among people where people had to delay their responses to trauma, such as a veteran who has just returned home, and their responses were perhaps delayed due to still being in a combat situation.

PTSD Means That You are Broken or Weak

PTSD is a mental condition that has nothing to do with how strong you are, and when you have PTSD, that also doesn't mean you are broken. You need to treat your PTSD, but it is not unlike having the flu in that you need to take time to recover, and PTSD is not your fault. You can't control if PTSD develops, and it doesn't speak to your character or your core self when you develop it. Some people are more at risk, but anyone who has trauma can get this. Fighting PTSD requires strength, and while it may make you feel weak, that's a myth that's perpetuated by PTSD and society at large. You cannot help your body's responses to traumatic stimuli, and all of PTSD is an involuntary response, so don't belittle yourself or others because of this condition.

PTSD Will Go Away If You Wait it Out

There are many reasons that people with PTSD may be wary of treatment, and it's normal to fear making such big changes. When you start to treat yourself, you have to address thoughts that may be hard for you to think about, let alone process. Therefore, it often seems easier to push those feelings away, but by pushing them away, you fuel the mechanisms that allow PTSD to thrive. Nevertheless, treatment is important because PTSD can linger for a long time and worsen when it is not treated. In some cases, PTSD can improve without assistance, but you cannot expect that such a case will happen for you. Finding professional help as well as choosing to learn the tools in this book will help you overcome your PTSD.

You Have to Experience an Exact List of Symptoms to Have PTSD

There are many symptoms that are commonly associated with PTSD, and while there are diagnostic criteria for PTSD, not all the symptoms will manifest in the same way, and you don't have to have all the symptoms listed to have PTSD. Each person responds to trauma differently, which means that they experience PTSD differently. Of the four clusters of symptoms, there is a wide range of potential side-effects that fall under each cluster, showing how diverse PTSD can appear among various people.

PTSD Only Impacts Veterans

People often associate PTSD with combat veterans, but that couldn't be further from the truth. Any trauma can cause PTSD, no matter what position a person is in. Veterans are at risk, but natural disasters, violence, and other hard events can also cause PTSD. Children are also at a huge risk for PTSD. After the terrorist attacks on 9/11, even children who just watched the events on TV were at risk for PTSD, and these rates increased the more the children watched TV. Young children were at increased risk than older children. What this information shows is that even just witnessing a traumatic event can lead to PTSD. Thus, its impact extends far beyond veterans.

PTSD Equals Violence

Too often, in pop culture and in the media, PTSD is associated with violence, which is harmful to sufferers of PTSD. It's true that people with PTSD may become violent, but that is not the norm; yet, it is a common portrayal. Violence is not itself a symptom of PTSD, but some of the symptoms may exacerbate violent tendencies. Usually, when violence does rarely occur in PTSD, that violence is not stemming from a want to be violent; rather, it is a defensive response to fear and a desire to self-protect. Further, substance abuse has been shown to worsen violent reactions in people with PTSD because it may amplify the worries and reactions of those who are suffering from PTSD. Accordingly, violence is not the usual state of people with PTSD, and assuming that is the case stigmatizes the illness.

Trauma and PTSD are the Same

While people with PTSD have trauma, not everyone who has trauma will develop PTSD. PTSD share a lot of emotional reactions and feelings, but PTSD is a mental health condition while trauma is something that regularly happens to people and creates a wide range of response. Trauma and PTSD are often used in conversation with one another, but it is erroneous to say they are the same. More on these key differences to come.

Defining PTSD

As the name would imply, PTSD is a condition that some people deal with because they have continued stress after a traumatic incident. PTSD is a mental condition, which means that it impacts the mental processes that sufferers have, and it can make it hard for them to function in ideal ways. While it is a mental health condition, it can also have several physical symptoms that further complicate the condition. While many people do experience negative side effects after having a traumatic experience, PTSD lasts for several weeks, and when untreated, it can endure much longer and take a serious toll on the experiences and relationships of the sufferer. It's best to get treatment as soon as the symptoms start to develop.

PTSD is generally diagnosed when you have experienced the symptoms for at least one month. These symptoms usually show up within one month of the trauma, but this time frame can vary. The DSM-5 outlines several behaviors that are required for a diagnosis. There are eight criteria, ranging from Criterion A to Criterion H. These criteria outline the kinds of symptoms and duration of symptoms that you need to have for a PTSD diagnosis. To get an official diagnosis, you need to seek a professional, but outlined below are the general categories for PTSD diagnosis.

Generally, practitioners diagnosis PTSD using the DSM-V. Symptoms are classified into the following groups that are required for diagnosis using the DSM-V:

> ➢ Criterion A: Stressor (the traumatic event)

➢ Criterion B: Intrusion Symptoms (re-experiencing the events through things like flashbacks, dreams, or memories)

➢ Criterion C: Avoidance (avoiding traumatic thoughts or things and people related to the trauma)

➢ Criterion D: Negative Alterations in Mood (worsened mood after the event with two symptoms in this category, such as distorted beliefs, amnesia, distorted blame, negative emotions, alienation, lack of enjoyment, or inability to feel positive emotions)

➢ Criterion E: Alterations in Arousal and Reactivity (two or more reactive responses changing as a result of trauma, such as recklessness and self-destruction, sleep issues, struggle focusing, startling easily, hypervigilance, or aggression and moodiness

➢ Criterion F: Symptoms of B, C, D, and E persist for at least one month

➢ Criterion G: Symptoms impair various areas of life

➢ Criterion H: The symptoms cannot be explained by other causes like sickness or the use of substances

If you have the symptoms listed, you should seek help as soon as you can so that you can get a professional diagnosis and start on your road towards recovery, using both therapy and the many methods provided in this book. Are you feeling overwhelmed? Don't worry; this book will guide you through the process and give you all the resources you need to get going on recovery.

How PTSD is Different from Trauma

While PTSD includes trauma, trauma and PTSD are not the same because the way you interact with them and what defines them is so different. Trauma refers to a disturbing event that happens to a person, but to have trauma, it doesn't matter the extent of how that trauma impacts you; a traumatic event will create a response, and no matter how short or long that response is, it is still trauma. Trauma is also a normal life experience. Most people will experience trauma, but most people do not experience PTSD. PTSD, further, is a mental health condition, which means that it causes disorder in people's lives, and many people can't get over it without a concentrated effort. Thus, not only does the experience of these two things differ, but the progression of these conditions differs as well.

Trauma isn't always PTSD, but PTSD always includes trauma. When you experience trauma, you have about a twenty percent chance of developing PTSD, which is higher than the at-large statistics; yet, this statistic shows that only about a fifth of traumas will trigger PTSD, so these terms are very far from being the same. PTSD is the result of a traumatic incident, but the key point of PTSD is that the person doesn't heal from the trauma and cope with it. Instead, they turn to unhealthy and unhealing coping mechanisms. More than that, PTSD causes people to respond to stimuli in other ways automatically. The brain works differently in a person with PTSD, which causes side effects.

Trauma becomes PTSD when it interferes with your daily life for a prolonged time. While you may have severe symptoms after a traumatic event has occurred, when those symptoms persist for several weeks after the trauma, there's a high likelihood that you have developed PTSD. If you've been experiencing symptoms for a month or more, there is a good chance that you have more than just trauma and that you have post-traumatic stress disorder. Duration and intensity are both factors that separate PTSD from normal trauma. When you struggle to enjoy normal things that give you joy because of your symptoms, your trauma may have become PTSD.

Unfortunately, trauma can easily become PTSD if you don't have a handle on that trauma. To reduce that risk, you should try to tackle your mental health when trauma happens. Try not to push the traumatic incident aside and push through it. There will be incidents where you're unable to stop the PTSD symptoms, but even when PTSD has developed, you can create a better relationship with yourself and work through the issues that fuel that PTSD and allow your symptoms to impede your life.

Who PTSD Impacts

While PTSD can impact anyone, there are certain people who are most at risk for PTSD. If you or a loved one are in one of these groups, you should always be extra mindful after traumatic events because such events could trigger PTSD or worsen existing PTSD. When you know you are at risk, you can better understand how PTSD impacts you, and hopefully, you can start to realize that you are in good company and are far from alone in your PTSD struggle. People everywhere, people just like you, are struggling right now, but people like you are also fighting to get better.

Certain groups of people may be prone to higher rates of PTSD. According to the Recovery Village, while men tend to have more trauma, women have significantly higher rates of PTSD. The National Center for PTSD has estimated that women were over two times as likely as men to have PTSD during their lifetimes. Among adults, middle-aged people from 45 to 59 were the most likely to have PTSD, and adults over 60 had the lowest occurrence of PTSD, according to Harvard Medical School. Additionally, several studies have connected race and PTSD, and they found that despite reporting fewer traumatic events, African Americans, Asian Americans, and Native Americans were more likely to have PTSD after experiencing trauma, which may be exasperated by societal conditions. These various groups may be prone, but there's still no telling who will develop PTSD and who will not, but it gives people an idea of what groups may need the most support post-trauma.

Childhood trauma is a major risk factor for PTSD. While most of the time, children are able to bounce back from trauma, millions of trauma experience PTSD. This PTSD can stem from a wide range of incidents, and many of the causes are the same as the causes adults face, but children may especially be at risk in the face of things like witnessing or experiencing violence, any kind of abuse or neglect, a death in the family, accidents, disasters, and bullying. Children are especially at risk for complex PTSD as well, and complex PTSD usually stems from prolonged childhood trauma, and this kind of PTSD complicates symptoms and treatment.

There is also a genetic risk that makes people more prone to PTSD. Scientists at the University of California San Diego (with the help of several other institutions) completed the largest and most diverse study on the genetic links of PTSD. The study showed that PTSD is "highly polygenic," which means that it is linked to many genetic variants. What all that means is that the genetic component of PTSD is as strong as it is in conditions like depression or anxiety. While more research needs to occur to find better predictive methods based on DNA, this research creates an important link between genetics and the development of PTSD. As a result, if you have family members with PTSD, you're at a higher risk of having PTSD yourself, which doesn't mean you will develop it, but it's something to be aware of.

Many situations create various odds of developing PTSD. In general, violence makes people prone to PTSD. Not only does experiencing violence cause PTSD, but witnessing violence can cause people to experience PTSD. Children and teens who witness violence are especially likely to develop PTSD, and prolonged violence can be especially harmful. Likewise, adults who see or experience violence may also be triggered. Seeing someone else be killed or injured has over a seven percent rate of PTSD, according to the Sidran Institute. Being physically assaulted, meanwhile, has a thirty-two percent PTSD rate, whereas a natural disaster only has just under four percent rate. Serious car accidents, stabbings or shootings, and unexpected deaths of loved ones all have around a fifteen percent or higher rate of PTSD. Thus, a wide range of issues can cause PTSD, and these examples are just some of the options.

One of the highest risk factors for PTSD is experiencing sexual violence. People who have been raped have a nearly fifty percent rate of PTSD, which is astronomical. Further, sufferers of other types of sexual assault also have high rates of PTSD, and just under twenty-four percent of people who experience those attacks get PTSD. Overall statistics of sexual assault suggest that forty-five percent of all survivors experience PTSD. Even in the absence of fully blown PTSD, seventy percent of survivors of sexual assault experience high levels of trauma. Accordingly, any type of sexual trauma is among the highest risk factors for PTSD.

Certain careers may increase your risk of PTSD. Veterans are another group that is well-known for developing PTSD. Additionally, first responders are also more likely to develop PTSD because of the stressful nature of their jobs and the traumatic incidents that they may witness. While the rate of PTSD among veterans varies based on era, the rates are anywhere from eleven to thirty percent. The type of warfare and the place where the war is fought are some of the factors that can increase PTSD. The Vietnam War, for example, has an up to thirty percent PTSD rate, perhaps due to guerilla warfare. Sexual assault also has a unique dynamic in a military setting as well, and as you know, this trauma has high rates of PTSD occurrence. Around twenty-three percent of women in the military reported sexual assault, and many cases go unreported. Further, in the military, a substantial thirty-eight percent and a starling fifty-five percent of women have faced sexual harassment, which can also be traumatic. Thus, not only does the combat and intense workplace of people in realms such as the military or police force impact their PTSD rates, but other systematic issues in organizations can also cause problems.

People who already have mental health issues are also vulnerable to PTSD. When you either have previous traumatic incidents or mental health issues, you're already vulnerable, so adding other trauma on top of that can be debilitating. Further, if you already struggle to cope, it's naturally going to be harder to take on more stress, and you have less mental space to process whatever events have happened to you. Further, if new trauma resembles old trauma, old wounds may be opened, which increases your chance of PTSD.

Your social connections can also make you more or less prone to PTSD. People who don't have a strong support system may struggle to process traumatic events on their own. Further, a weak support system may make them resistant to healthy coping tools that would help them address their trauma. Some social environments, for example, discourage emotional responses and encourage people to push down their emotions, and these kinds of attitudes can allow PTSD symptoms to creep into your life. Having a good support system is vital for anyone who is going through hardship. While you can survive without a support system, you cannot thrive on your own. Thus, your support system can influence how your trauma develops and whether or not it becomes PTSD.

Studies are already starting to evaluate how COVID-19 is impacting levels of PTSD. While the research is still young, one Italian study showed that thirty percent of people who survived COVID-19 had PTSD after their recovery. Women with COVID-19 developed PTSD more commonly, as did people who were delirious or agitated when they were sick with COVID-19. The people with PTSD also tended to have more lasting medical systems, even as they were better. Beyond just those who have experienced COVID-19 themselves, many psychological professionals are prepared for significant rates of PTSD caused by COVID-19. The societal challenges, such as quarantining and safety measures, could cause psychological ramifications, as can the massive loss of life and the fear that came along with the pandemic. More research will need to be done, but the global pandemic was a trauma that people jointly experienced and will continue to experience the impacts of COVID-19 for quite some time.

Each case of PTSD will be individual, but if you or a loved one have experienced some of the more common risk factors, it's important to evaluate your symptoms and try to determine if traumatic events have caused reoccurring trauma. But what are the symptoms, and how do these symptoms impact the lives of people with PTSD?

Symptoms of PTSD

We've touched on the requirements of diagnosis, but this section will flesh out those symptoms and help you understand them better. The symptoms of PTSD are varied, but when you learn to recognize these symptoms, you can learn to spot the red flags of PTSD. You don't have to have all these symptoms to have PTSD. Further, your symptoms may expand beyond the common symptoms, so if you don't feel like yourself and you've experienced trauma, it's worth investigating your responses and seeking a professional to see if you do have PTSD. A diagnosis itself won't fix the problems you face but knowing whether your trauma has caused a disorder gives you a place to start, and knowing the symptoms can help you catch your PTSD or the PTSD of loved ones early.

There are several mental symptoms that you may experience when you have PTSD, and many of these symptoms may overlap with the ones you experience when you are stressed, but they are rooted in your trauma and are often magnified by that trauma. Re-experiencing trauma is one of the most prominent symptoms of PTSD, and you may have memories or flashbacks that intrude on your normal thinking and interrupt your day. It's also normal for people to dissociate when they have these responses, which means that they feel detachment from themselves or the present moment. Nightmares are also a common occurrence. People with PTSD may also have comorbid conditions, such as depression, anxiety, or substance abuse, and these conditions can make it harder to improve the PTSD symptoms.

PTSD sometimes causes people to avoid certain things. You may stay away from things that you know will remind you of your trauma, including certain situations, people, places, and objects. This avoidance can cause you to eliminate things from your life that make you happy. For example, if a person you love reminds you of your trauma, you may avoid them even though you enjoy being with them, and they could be a good support system for you.

While PTSD can result in avoidance, others may become more confrontational. You may startle more easily and feel that you are always on edge. You can't relax, and you may feel wired. People may feel more aggravated and moody. Additionally, PTSD can induce reckless behaviors. All these surging emotions can make it hard for people with PTSD to focus or even sleep.

PTSD can also change the way you look at yourself. You may become more critical of yourself and start to think that you are a bad person. You may forget certain things, and this kind of amnesia is normal in people with PTSD because your brain is trying to protect itself from the trauma. Further, just as you could blame other people for your situation, you could blame yourself. Shame and fear are also common emotions that may stem from your PTSD. Others feel guilt or anger in excess.

You may also have physical responses, such as a quickened heart rate or shaky hands. Stimuli, such as loud noises (fireworks, a car backfiring, etc.) or certain smells, may trigger flashbacks and fight or flight responses. People with PTSD may feel more fatigue, headaches, muscle aches, and general sickness.

You should note that children may have unique symptoms. For example, some children may act out their trauma as they are playing. They might also have intense dreams, but these dreams aren't necessarily about the event itself (though they might be). They might generally complain of feeling sick despite not having an underlining condition, so it might seem like they're just trying to skip school. Additionally, children may become more fearful of leaving their parents, and they may follow their parents around. They may become angry or restless, and it might be hard to get them to focus on activities they normally enjoyed. It's also common for children to cry more or have more meltdowns.

The symptoms of PTSD vary in intensity, and as you continue to suffer from PTSD, they may change over time based on your continued experiences and coping mechanisms. There are many stigmas associated with PTSD, such as sufferers being violent or otherwise dangerous. However, looking at the full extent of symptoms, it's clear that those stigmas are overblown. While PTSD can result in violent behaviors, there is so much more to the condition than that, and people with PTSD can live normal, well-adjusted lives, especially when their symptoms are treated with care and understanding rather than judgment.

Four Stages of PTSD

Some scholars use four stages as a framework to show how PTSD may develop and progress, as detailed by Pyramid Health. While reiterating the fact that individuals experience PTSD differently, there's a common progression that represents many cases of PTSD, which can show sufferers generally what to expect as well as help give perspective to those who have loved ones with PTSD. Not everyone will go through all of these stages, but it is normal if you do. Recovery from PTSD isn't easy, and it will have many ups and downs, but by being ready for these ups and downs, you can better stay on track and avoid becoming so discouraged that you resign yourself to being unhappy and traumatized forever.

Impact

The first stage of PTSD is the impact stage, sometimes called the "emergency" stage. It is called this because it happens right after the trauma has happened (or as the PTSD starts to develop in delayed cases). It catapults the sufferer into their PTSD, and it can take a while for this stage to build up. During this stage, the person with PTSD is just starting to deal with the ramifications of the trauma. They are passing the shock, and at this point, the person is probably incredibly anxious. They are often hypervigilant and generally on edge. They are having a hard time processing the events that have happened to them, so they aren't at the point where they can even fully rationalize the events. The emotions are just starting to settle, which can make this a tumultuous and confusing stage for suffers.

Denial

One of the hardest stages to combat is the denial stage. Many people don't want to admit that anything is wrong, and they don't want to confront the intense feelings that they are experiencing, so they push the trauma away and try to deny it. Unfortunately, denial doesn't make the pain go away, nor does it solve PTSD, and in some cases, it can make it worse. During this stage, the negative feelings continue to build despite the denial, and strong emotions will continue to cause side effects. Not everyone is in denial during recovery, but it is one of the more common reactions because people would rather pretend they are fine or that they can manage their trauma rather than confront their issues. During this stage, you may be more prone to substance abuse as people often want to try to numb out their emotions as a way of avoiding them.

Short-Term Recovery

The short-term recovery stage requires people to create solutions for their most pressing issues. This stage has sufferers address their most immediate issues, and it allows them to start to get back to normal. The hardships of PTSD will linger in this stage, but this stage gives coping tools and techniques that allow the person with PTSD to start to get themselves back and mediate their symptoms even if some of those symptoms persist for a while. Short-term recovery is important, but patients with PTSD must also evaluate their long-term recovery goals to avoid relapse and keep the normalcy they have created in this stage.

Long-Term Recovery

The long-term recovery stage requires a person to continue to deal with their PTSD. Even when most of the symptoms are gone, a person still may have rough periods. Certain events can be retraumatizing, or stress may bring the symptoms back out. Some people will completely beat their PTSD, but for others, continued practice of techniques and skills learned will be vital for long-term well-being. It's okay to need this long-term recovery, and any lingering symptoms don't reflect on your effort or dignity as a person.

Complex PTSD

Complex PTSD, also known as C-PTSD, is a condition that has an overlap of symptoms with PTSD, but it also has some additional symptoms of its own. It is not its own condition in the DSM-V; yet, distinguishing when PTSD is complex can help clinicians and individuals better treat PTSD and get to the root of the issue. Further, many clinicians believe that it is very different than PTSD and needs to be handled differently in treatment. Even so, researchers only began to learn about the conditions in the eighties; thus, there's still a lot to discover about its nuances.

What sets C-PTSD apart is the fact that it stems from repeated trauma. Complex PTSD is often more intense because it occurs in people who have had prolonged trauma. For example, a child who grows up in an abusive household may develop PTSD after being in a traumatic environment for years. Childhood trauma is normal for those with C-PTSD. Complex PTSD most commonly develops from childhood traumatic experiences; though, there are some exceptions.

The trauma that causes C-PTSD may last for months or even years, which complicates the trauma simply because of the scope of the trauma. The trauma then becomes harder to pinpoint, which then also impacts the treatment plan for someone with that kind of pain.

Some of the causes for complex PTSD include domestic violence or witnessing violence in general. In any case that a child feels unsafe, especially at the hands of someone who is supposed to protect them, they are at risk for complex PTSD because children are often helpless, meaning that they rely on guardians to look after their well-being, and when that doesn't happen, it shakes their expectations and perception of the world at large. Accordingly, parental abandonment, abuse, or neglect could trigger C-PTSD. Child displacement, such as being in foster care, may also put a child at risk. Violence within a country can also have a profound impact, and C-PTSD is often experienced by child soldiers, slaves, or people who have experienced genocide. The main thread in these circumstances is that the sufferers were helpless and could not escape the traumatic events that surrounded them.

Complex PTSD has the same fundamental side effects as PTSD, but these side effects may manifest in slightly different ways. For example, a person's relationship with their sense of self may be more impacted by C-PTSD. A person may falter when asked about their values or core beliefs. They may lose faith in religion or feel hopeless about the world. People with this condition may also detach themselves from the pain they feel through depersonalization and derealization, or they may forget the traumatic events altogether. Additionally, people with C-PTSD are especially prone to having a negative self-image. They may feel guilt, shame, or helplessness. Further, they may struggle to regulate their emotions and may be quick to anger, susceptible to sadness, or even have suicidal or depressive thoughts. C-PTSD can also be debilitating for relationships, and those with this condition may struggle to have healthy relationships, or they may stay away from forming relationships altogether. These symptoms can be incredibly painful, but they can also make it hard for people with complex PTSD to live their lives in satisfying ways.

CHAPTER 3

THE BRAIN AND TRAUMA

I f you want to understand the effect of unhealed trauma on your mind, you should have a basic knowledge of how the brain operates. The brain is a complex organ that controls your bodily functions and your reactions. Your brain does its best to take information and lead you to the best decisions possible, but your brain is not perfect because it is not omniscient, and despite its best efforts, it doesn't always properly interpret information, and its interpretation can shift based on your experiences, which shape your brain's behavior. The functioning and even the structure of your brain can change because of PTSD, and that sounds scary, but fortunately, once you know what you are up against, you can start to work with your brain's natural structure and use that to your advantage. The brain is far from simple, and there's still a lot to learn about it, but what we do know is highly illuminating.

Two Brain Systems: A Straightforward Way of Understanding Your Thoughts

You've probably heard of some of the more well-known parts of the brain, like the prefrontal cortex or the amygdala. You might've heard terms like "the reptilian brain" or the "thinking brain," and if you've heard these terms before, you've already got some idea of some of the complex parts of the brain. With so many parts of the brain, it feels like you have to be a neuroscientist to understand it all, but this book starts out generally and then becomes more specific so that you can understand the basic concepts before you're asked to understand a bunch of parts, many of which that have similar but nuanced roles in your thinking.

One key brain functioning is your thought processes and how those processes lead to actions. While you choose to do many things each day, a good amount of what you do is subconscious. At the University of Southern California, research led by Wendy Wool suggests that around forty-five percent of our actions are habitual behaviors, and when you get stressed or busy, it's normal for your habitual behaviors to kick in and take over. When you have good habits, those habits can lead to you making healthier decisions under pressure, while bad habits can worsen your side effects and make it harder to function. Habitual behaviors rule nearly half of our lives, so they have a huge impact on your well-being, and more than that, when you learn more about how your brain and unconscious thoughts function, it becomes easier to confront your trauma and create habits that heal that trauma rather than avoid or worsen it.

If the way the brain works is a little overwhelming for you to understand, it will help to look at the brain more broadly before we start to pinpoint specific parts of the brain. One of the easiest ways is to think of your brain as having two systems. In his book, *Thinking Fast and Slow*, Daniel Kahneman uses this framework as he breaks the human brain down into two systems, each of which are composed of various parts of the brain that we will discuss some more going forward. These systems control both your unconscious and your conscious thoughts, both of which are important in your decision-making and how you react to stimuli. With this information, Kahneman clearly delineates how your unconscious and conscious decisions relate to one another using his two systems.

His first system is a group of parts of the brain that Kahneman lumps together as System 1. System 1 is the automatic part of your brain. Think of an animal in the wild when you think of this system. The first system represents your animalistic drive for survival. This part of the brain also represents "fast thinking," meaning that you come to conclusions instantaneously. System 1 is what allows you to know that one plus one is two without having to stop to calculate. It's been drilled into your head so much that it is automatic. This thinking is unconscious. These are your automatic reactions. When someone swings an arm at you, you may duck to avoid getting hit, or you may flinch in fear without meaning to do so. This part of your brain isn't just a pre-programmed human instinct.

A big chunk of this system is learned experience. Trauma can, therefore, have a strong impact on this part of your brain. If you are in a car accident after someone ran a red light, you may become hyper-vigilant at red lights and respond in instinctual ways in that scenario, even if there aren't "logical." Imagine a buff man being yelled at by a much smaller man; logically, the buff man would know that he could take the other in a fight if he needed to, but if that smaller man reminds the buff man of his abusive father, the buff man may automatically respond in fear when the smaller man starts yelling because past experience dictates that yelling leads to eventual pain for the buff man.

The second system is conscious thinking. Your System 2 brain is notoriously lethargic, and it is no wonder. It takes more time and energy to use system two, so when System 1 can be used, it's better. It's why your morning routine is generally the same, and often, you probably go through your morning without much thought. You're falling back on automatic processes because you're too tired to think too hard about things that you've done many times before. Moreover, System 1 decisions are often the safer choices. Humans have learned that habitual behaviors are not only more efficient, but they are safer, and they help us survive. It's why we are creatures of habits! Habits are behaviors that we have well tested. We feel more sure of the results of habitual behaviors because, in our experience, those things have consistently worked to make our lives better (or at least make us *feel* better, and some habits give us relief but are overall unhealthy). System 2 is more of a gamble. We can use our best judgment, but good analysis and things that are out of the norm never feel as safe as the comfort zone our habits create.

Slow and lazy, your conscious brain doesn't want to do anything if it doesn't have to. When given the option, System 2 defers judgment to System 1, but there are times when you need to use this brain because System 1 cannot give adequate judgments, requiring System 2 to do some digging and start analytical processes. When you look at the math problem 345 + 4673, you cannot solve the problem right away. Even people who are good at math have to quickly add the problem up. System 2 can be quick. Not every calculation takes several minutes, but it is not instantaneous. You have to search your brain for things you know and try to use that information to come up with a decision. When you have to make a lot of these analytical decisions, you may feel exhausted. Conscious decisions are hard, and System 1 decisions are often a shortcut, but shortcuts aren't always better in the long run, even if they save us time!

System 1 is the survival part of your brain. Humans have been conditioned for survival, and they have evolved to take on the challenges that they face in their lives. Thus, you have System 1 because, in early times, our species had to live in a dangerous world. We didn't have nice houses to shelter us and any degree of separation from nature. We lived among nature, and doing so was vital for our survival. To survive, we had to develop fight-or-flight instincts. Having to stop to weigh the pros and cons of a situation could very easily lead to death. If someone throws a rock at you, you don't stop to spend five minutes deciding whether to catch the rock or to duck. You act right away because, by the time the five minutes passed, you would already have been hit by that rock! Your System 1 brain steps in when you need to think fast, which is either in an urgent scenario or when you're doing something that you've done a million times before. Sometimes, this system acts too impulsively. It steps in when the situation isn't all that dangerous. Human lives are incredibly different than they were when our survival instincts formed and because System 1 doesn't have the time or resources to analyze, all it can do is rely on instincts and what has come before.

As you know, habits are formed in the subconscious part of your brain, and they are shaped by your past experiences. For example, if you get hit in the head after failing to catch a rock tumbling towards you, you might duck the next time, knowing that trying to catch the rock got you hurt before. This concept applies specifically to PTSD. Your System 1 brain frantically tries to protect you from things that have hurt you in the past, including your trauma. For instance, your instincts may encourage you to run away from your issues— your flight mode activated— and you may have learned early on that it's easy to push those issues aside than confront them. Confrontation is scary, and your body may resist that confrontation, even if logically you know you need to address your issues to feel better. While habitual behaviors are subconscious, and you do them before you can stop and think about the ramifications, that doesn't mean that those behaviors are unchangeable. In fact, you can use your System 2 brain to consciously make changes to old habits; it takes time, but when you replace old, unhealthy coping skills with better skills, you'll start to see a difference in your overall mindset.

Meanwhile, System 2 has unique properties of its own that you can use to your advantage when you have PTSD. System 2 enables you to create awareness. You can catch yourself acting on a habit. For example, maybe there's a certain situation that reminds you of your trauma. You might become angry whenever such a situation happens. You might yell at a loved one in frustration and fear without thinking about it. Later, when you have time to reflect, you feel guilty for your behavior. While you may want to shrug off the moment and try to forget that it happened at all, it could benefit you more to reflect on what happened and why you felt the way that you did at that moment. When you become aware of these details, you can start to act in new ways when confronted with those same feelings. Knowing your tendencies and building new automatic thought processes is one of the most powerful parts of your System 2 brain, and it allows you to recover from the trauma that has hurt you.

If you want to shift your habitual behaviors, it is best to use both of your systems in conjunction because neither part of your brain can work alone. If you used your System 2 brain for everything, it would take forever to make basic decisions like what way to drive to work in the morning or how to make your coffee! Likewise, if you only used your System 1 brain, you'd be living like a wild animal. You'd have no ability to rationalize. All you would have were your instinctual knowledge, which is very limited, and it wouldn't allow you to do some of the things that make you feel human and that make you human. Human reasoning is part of humanity, and making conscious decisions is also a huge part of your day— over half of all decisions. Your systems work best when you use them together, lessening the weaknesses of each one and highlighting the strength.

While you may feel powerless to your brain sometimes, the truth is that you're the one with the power. Your brain works using the information that you give it. You can influence your thought process. Even with simple steps like thinking more positively, you can influence your subconscious behaviors. Of course, PTSD is a complex disorder that you can't cure just by thinking more positively, but such methods can ease your symptoms and give you a clearer mindset as you work through your issues. Further, they can make it easier to deal with the hard truths you may have to face as you get better.

The Triune Brain

We're going to continue to build your knowledge of the brain by exploring the triune brain. Now that you've learned about two systems of thinking, it's time to look at the brain in three parts. While Kahneman focuses on thinking speed in his depiction, McClean focuses on three types of regulation facilitated by your brain-body regulation, emotional regulation, and thought regulation. In 1970,

Paul McClean coined the term "triune" brain to explain the division of our brain's everyday functions into three equal parts.

According to McClean, we have a three-part triune brain where there is a reptilian brain (hindbrain) regulating our body, the mammalian brain (midbrain) regulating our emotions, and the thinking brain (neomammalian brain) regulating our thinking. Ideally, all three parts of the brain are communicating with each other and are working together. Your limbic system, brainstem, and cortex are some of the predominant parts of the triune brain.

Each part of your brain has unique functions that kick into action under different circumstances. Your brain ideally works together harmoniously, and each part plays its role without friction, but unfortunately, that's not always the case, and while your brain always acts the way it was wired, certain stimuli can make your brain act in ways that don't reflect your best interests. Your brain sometimes even acts in ways that frustrate and scare you, as is often the case with PTSD—lifting the mystery around how your brain works, therefore, can be comforting people who are confounded by their PTSD.

Reptilian Brain

First, there is the reptilian brain or the hindbrain. This part of the brain includes the brainstem and cerebellum. This part of your brain is at the top of your spinal cord, where your neck is based, and it governs behaviors that are the unconscious, commonly automatic processes that you never think about. For instance, it deals with your fight or flight response (more on this later), and it also deals with your physiological functions, your breathing, and your pulse.

These responses are vital in understanding your PTSD and the automatic responses that result.

The Mammalian Brain

The midbrain is also important to understand a little bit about when you are learning to deal with trauma. This system includes the limbic system, which is also known as the "emotional" brain. It is located underneath the cerebral cortex and above the brainstem. The limbic system is several parts of your brain that operate collaboratively. The parts of this brain include the thalamus, amygdala, hippocampus, and hypothalamus. This part of your brain deals with your emotional processes.

Thinking Brain

The third region of the brain is the forebrain and the cortex. In literature, this part of the brain is sometimes nicknamed the "thinking brain." As the name would imply, this section of the brain is where thinking, reasoning, and cognition take place. If the amygdala is the emotional part of the brain, the cortex is the rational part. In the frontal lobe, your prefrontal cortex is nestled just behind your forehead and has three overarching functions.

The first is regulating your amygdala's responses and the emotions related to those responses. The prefrontal cortex is the part of your brain that guides you through decisions. It also slows things down when you start to understand that something you're afraid of isn't threatening you. Your prefrontal cortex can be ignored when other parts of your brain take over, and when that happens, it will be harder for you to rationalize your fear and deal with it. Thus, you may be in a reactive state even when you're not in danger. You may also be more emotional in general.

Another duty of your thinking brain relates to memory. You have memories based on the processing of your senses that your brain encodes using the details it can gather. You have a limited perception, so your memory isn't always accurate. Your prefrontal cortex is one of the most important areas of your brain in this respect because it connects the dots between the data you connect, and it forms the narrative that you have about your experiences.

The final role that we'll discuss here of the prefrontal cortex is that it helps you with focus. You will struggle to focus if this part of your brain isn't as engaged as you need it to be. This lack of focus can make it hard for your brain to encode things into memory, and thus, you may forget things when your prefrontal cortex isn't working strongly and is overridden.

Thus, all these functions can be shifted among people who have PTSD. One specific area that is often impacted is the inferior frontal gyrus, which is the lowest gyrus of the frontal lobe. This part of the brain and some of the others related to impulse tend to have lessened cortical thickness in people with PTSD. Thus, as a result, people with PTSD may be more prone to impulsive and high-risk behaviors.

Key Parts of the Brain

The following section will break down the parts of the brain even further, and it will highlight some of the parts and systems in the brain that most influence PTSD and how research has shown those areas are impacted after trauma and in those who suffer from PTSD as opposed to non-PTSD brains.

The Thalamus

The thalamus is a part of your brain that is on the stem. It is sometimes known as a gatekeeper because the senses go through this part of your brain as they process. During times of danger, the thalamus is the part of your brain that is going through sensory data so that it can then go to the amygdala, which deals with your fight or flight response.

The Amygdala

The almond-shaped part of your brain called the amygdala sits about an inch past your eyes, near the hippocampus. Thus, it is in the front of your temporal lobes. The amygdala is so important because it influences many of the processes that are linked to PTSD. You actually have one of these on each half of your brain, and each plays a specific function in how you process events. The amygdala is responsible for the flight response. The right amygdala deals with bad emotions, and the left deals with both good and bad emotions. Together, they regulate how you fear, and they help determine your emotional responses. The amygdala is geared to help you react quickly when your wellbeing is threatened.

One of the most important roles of the amygdala is to sense fear because fear is what tells your body to be prepared to act, and it allows you to override processes that may slow down your thinking during the times that urgency can mean life or death. The amygdala often overreacts to stimuli in people with PTSD. While fear doesn't feel good, it is important because it allows you to sense potentially dangerous situations before those situations hurt you. When you have PTSD, your amygdala may be in overdrive. When you sense certain things that remind you of your trauma, your amygdala often sets off your body's security system, which creates the physical and emotional response you get in fearful situations. It tells your body to emit chemicals, and that's why you can physically feel fear, and that's also why your amygdala may overreact in certain scenarios and make you fearful with those same physical symptoms, even though rationally you know you're not in danger.

Along with emotions, the amygdala determines which memories get stored in the brain. Again, this can influence your memory of traumatic events and be part of your PTSD, which commonly includes amnesia of traumatic events. The amygdala also weaves together your emotions and your memories. Experts think that the type of emotional response an event causes effects which memories get saved. Memories that have strong emotional meaning tend to stick, but when trauma is intense, your brain may block those memories. The amygdala can also cause hyper-vigilance. The amygdala sends signals to the prefrontal cortex, which determines whether or not the threat is over or if the body should stay alert. This part of the brain often becomes too active while the medial prefrontal cortex isn't active enough, meaning that PTSD suffers struggle to regain their calmness and normal functioning after a threatening incident.

Hippocampus

The hippocampus is linked to the amygdala, and it is a horseshoe-shaped lobe that curves back from the amygdala. The hippocampus is the key brain center for memory because it is responsible for turning short-term memory into long-term memory. It primarily retrieves memories, but it also helps you know the difference between a memory that happened in the past and what is currently happening to you.

While it is mostly responsible for storing and retrieving memories, it also differentiates between past and present experiences. The hippocampus is also a key brain structure for learning new things. Your hippocampus may not be doing its job properly when you are experiencing PTSD because you may struggle to tell the present from the past when you have a flashback or dissociative experience. This part of the brain can also impact how much you retain your memories, so you may have distorted recall related to your trauma because the hippocampus is in charge of putting things into context when you have fear, so it especially can impact memories related to trauma.

Hypothalamus

The hypothalamus is located just above the brainstem, and the important job of the hypothalamus is to maintain the status quo. This part of your brain collects information from across your body, and it sends signals to try to create homeostasis in your body. It collects information from each of your five senses, which all have a unique area in your brain. It can create a hormonal reaction that starts your fight or flight response, which causes you to revert to automatic responses rather than thoughtful decision-making. Accordingly, the hypothalamus reacts differently in people with PTSD, which can cause the stress response to be triggered more frequently.

Trauma and the Brain

Research shows that trauma is processed and stored in the limbic system. Trauma increases the activity in the amygdala. When a person experiences a traumatic event, adrenaline rushes through the body, and the memory is imprinted into the amygdala.

It's hard to think rationally when your amygdala is activated because your amygdala is trying to fight for your survival by making decisions as quickly as it can with the information it has already collected. It relies on past responses to shape current decisions. Things that helped you find safety before are what it will want to use again, even if those things aren't healthy or applicable to the current situation. The amygdala also results in your flight, fight, or freeze response (sometimes just known as your fight or flight response).

Fight-Flight-Freeze Response

In an emergency, your body must react promptly. The fight-flight-freeze response begins in your amygdala, as it is the part of your brain that perceives fear. This response is one of the most instinctual ones that humans have. When you sense danger is present or when under a lot of stress, your amygdala wants to automatically activate this response because the sooner it sends signals, the sooner you can respond to the danger. When the threat is serious, the amygdala acts quickly by triggering the fight or flight response because when in danger, you must act quickly.

You may not be able to think logically when this happens. A psychologist named Daniel Goleman dubbed this response the "amygdala hijack" in his 1995 book, *Emotional Intelligence: Why It Can Matter More Than IQ*. This hijack occurs when you are in a stressful situation, and your amygdala triggers your fight or flight response. It takes away your ability to think rationally and have full autonomy over your responses. You're in automatic mode, and you've lost manual control. Your fear causes you to focus on the animalistic part of your brain.

When this happens, you can often feel the shift in your brain. You may start to have a foggy or muddled feeling in your mind. You're in survival mode, and you struggle to think clearly and use your System 2 brain. You become dominated by your fear, and as the fear persists, you become unable to focus on other things because you are hyper-vigilant. Your brain is trying to keep you safe with the amygdala hijack, but when this response occurs more often than it should, it can interfere with your life, and it often takes a while to get back to thinking normally. Thus, this response can get in the way of your work, your home life, and in general, it lessens your ability to enjoy certain moments.

Some people don't fight or flight in response to trauma. Instead, some people will freeze in the face of danger instead and become paralyzed by their fear, and this response is actually the most usual response to trauma. You may feel your body become weak, or you may pass out. You may feel unable to move and lethargic because of this response. This is a normal reaction that is part of our brain's protective system.

Trauma and the Hippocampus

The relationship between the amygdala and the hippocampus cannot be overstated. When you go through a traumatic time, your amygdala gets in the way of your hippocampus and steps into its territory, basically. Some research shows that when you have persistent stress, your hippocampus is damaged because the hormone cortisol can destroy the cells in that region. Thus, the balance between your amygdala and your hippocampus becomes skewed.

Your hippocampus backs off a little when you have experienced trauma, which results in you struggling to differentiate between current events and the ones that have occurred in the past, and this symptom is common among people who have PTSD. Thus, people may have trauma reactions in circumstances that remind them of their trauma, even if those circumstances are not dangerous. For example, someone who was raped in a parking lot at night might feel fear and have a panic response in any parking lot. Likewise, a war veteran might remember a smell from combat, and similar smells may cause a fearful response. They may also hear a loud sound that reminds them of gunfire and react. These instances show how your hippocampal responses influence how your brain processes scenarios. You may feel like you are back to past experiences and lose track of what is presently happening.

When you experience trauma, the way you deal with memories changes. Sometimes, you will remember things more vividly, but on other occasions, you may experience amnesia and forget certain moments near or during the time you were traumatized. These memory issues can be painful and confusing for people with PTSD.

They can make it harder for you to process trauma and cause a lot of fear.

Often the hippocampus will affect the ability to recall some memories for trauma survivors—it like a computer memory that writes files to its hard drive. After a trauma, your hippocampus works to remember the event accurately and make sense of it. But because trauma is typically overwhelming, all the information doesn't get coded correctly. Your brain does its best, but there's only so much it can process at once, and it tries to prioritize information that it thinks could be most useful. This tendency means that you might have trouble remembering important details of the event, or you might find yourself thinking a lot about what happened because your hippocampus is working so hard to try to make sense of things.

This happens because the amygdala activates the HPA axis, resulting in a flood of neurohormones that interfere with hippocampal learning or the ability to write data files to your hard drive. This is why, after a stressful situation, people have trouble remembering some specific details and say things like, "It was all a blur."

This means that when someone is having a traumatic response or trying to recall memories of a traumatic event, they may not be able to recall details of the event, or their recall of the event may not be chronological or linear, which is called fragmented memory. Fragmented memory is a completely natural way of processing traumatic events. Your brain automatically tries to piece these memories together to make sense of them, but sometimes it has limited success, so you may feel a little confused or forget the details altogether.

The hippocampus widely impacts how you respond to trauma, and when you have PTSD, it continues to be in trauma mode, and it won't always react in a way that allows you to live your life how you would like to live your life.

Trauma and the Prefrontal Cortex

Your prefrontal cortex is another region that heavily impacts your PTSD, as I've mentioned a little bit before. Trauma can cause permanent or enduring changes in this part of your brain, which can balance the responses of your amygdala. Thus, when you have trauma, your stress response may be greater than it would normally be. You may feel increased fear and stress even when the stimuli don't connect back to your traumatic experiences. Normal things may make you feel hyper-vigilant. Research supports the idea that trauma commonly makes it hard for your prefrontal cortex to normalize your emotional responses. The trauma responses take over, which makes it hard for you to think clearly as the amygdala hijack occurs.

The Brain Impacts Trauma Intensely

Ultimately, the processes in your brain are the ones that dictate your PTSD and cause the mental and physical responses that you have with PTSD. Your brain is responsible for all your bodily processes, and it dictates both your emotional and physical responses. Thus, it is imperative that you understand at least the basics of these systems and how they relate to your PTSD because if you don't understand your brain, it's hard to rationalize how PTSD works or how you can heal it.

Seeing these processes also shows you that your condition is perfectly normal. You aren't broken, and your brain isn't broken either. It might not be working optimally, but with some tune-ups, you can get it back where it needs to be so that you're healthy and happy. Your brain is responding as it was wired to do so, and while it may be getting its signals mixed, learning skills and therapeutic techniques can help you feed your brain with more helpful stimuli. There is hope that you can get better, and as you'll see throughout this book, just as trauma can change your mind, so can post-traumatic growth.

CHAPTER 4

COPING WITH PTSD

The Importance of Coping Skills

Many coping skills are simple steps that people take to deal with that trauma. Most of these behaviors only take a few minutes a day, or even just a few minutes per week. You have to build several of these skills so that you have a range of options that will fit a variety of hard scenarios. When you take the time to create healthy coping skills, you invest in your well-being, and you start to combat the fears that may make it hard for you to enjoy your life. Alternatively, unhealthy coping skills have the opposite impact, which is why you need to learn about common coping skills and how to make them healthier.

Coping skills are like release valves. When you start to feel pressured, they kick in and let some of the excess energy out of your body. They make sure that you don't get too overwhelmed, and when you start to feel yourself spiraling, they are a toolbox that you can use to take charge of your mental processes. Coping skills are what keep people happy and healthy, even as they go through the hardships that life throws at them. Life will never be without bumps in the road, but it doesn't have to feel insurmountable. With coping skills, you feel in charge of your life, and you remember that you can handle whatever happens, even if you have to work hard to handle it. Your fear remains, but you find courage in your coping skills.

When you have coping skills, you are also better able to deal with your triggers. Triggers are one of the hardest parts of PTSD to deal with, and they can often happen unexpectedly. Small things can send you spiraling back to the trauma. They take you out of the moment, and they put you back to a place you never wanted to visit again. While coping skills cannot erase the trauma you have, they give you the knowledge you need to get through the hardest moments. You reduce your stress levels, and as a result, you also can reduce how much PTSD impacts your daily life.

If you don't build positive coping skills, you will probably fall back on negative ones that make you worse off. Neglecting positive coping skills always leads to bad coping skills because negative copings skills can seem so appealing. They seem like easy fixes, and often they make you feel good for a while, even when they do nothing to help you. Resist the temptation to fall into that trap. If you already have negative coping skills, it's time to combat those skills so that you can change your relationship with your PTSD.

It can be hard to deal with all the challenges of the world, especially as you are dealing with your trauma. Normal life can set back your progress when you become overwhelmed and don't know how to deal with all the problems that never seem to stop in life. Fear not; the solution isn't as arduous as you think. By taking a few minutes a day to practice healthy coping, you can transform your life, and those coping skills will help you get through the hardships of normal

COPING WITH PTSD

life as you start to address your trauma, a process that can take a good amount of time.

Unhealthy Coping Mechanisms How to Combat Them

Unfortunately, many people with PTSD turn to unhealthy coping mechanisms as they try to deal with the ramifications of the trauma they experienced. These coping mechanisms may be things that the person is aware are harmful to them, but they may feel powerless to change these mechanisms because, while maladaptive, these mechanisms provide emotional relief or temporarily help the person deal with symptoms. In any case, these methods do not help the person's PTSD long-term, and using unhealthy coping methods can even cause more harm and delay recovery. If you suffer from PTSD, you may use several of these, and part of recovery is learning how to fight these tendencies and apply healthier mechanisms. Further, even if you don't have any of these yet, it still helps to be aware of behaviors to look out for. The sooner you catch them, the easier it is to break any bad habits you've formed.

Impulsive Actions

Another potential side effect of PTSD is reckless behavior. In general, you may be prone to things like compulsive shopping, binge eating, driving dangerously, excess drinking, or self-harm when you have PTSD. These behaviors can help you find temporary relief from painful emotions, and many of these behaviors cause chemical reactions in your body that temporarily make you feel better. This

— 73 —

category includes several unhealthy coping mechanisms, and it can present itself in a wide variety of ways.

To limit these impulsive behaviors, it is good to find replacement behaviors that make you feel good without being destructive. It also helps to remind yourself of the consequences of these actions when you feel an urge to do them. Just one conscious moment of awareness can break through the impulsive desire or at least interrupt it so that you can eventually begin to challenge it. You need to limit your impulsive behaviors to keep yourself safe and get on the path to recovery.

Substance Abuse

Substance abuse is one of the more prevalent comorbid conditions with PTSD because many PTSD sufferers use substances to numb their pain. These substances can be both legal and illegal, including alcohol, illicit drugs, and prescription drug abuse. According to the National Center for PTSD, 46.4% of people who had PTSD over their lifetimes also met the requirements for substance abuse disorder (additional people with PTSD abuse substances but do not meet the criteria for substance abuse disorder). Additional research showed that women experienced substance abuse disorder with PTSD at a rate of nearly 28 percent, while men experienced it at a rate of 51.9 percent. Further, these rates are even higher in veterans. Vietnam War veterans have especially high rates, and 74 percent of Vietnam veterans who had PTSD also qualified for a substance abuse disorder. Across research, substance abuse stands out among PTSD sufferers. These statistics clearly show substance abuse is an appealing and destructive coping mechanism for people with PTSD.

People who are dealing with trauma need to be careful around substances, even if they don't have a history of substance abuse. Substance abuse can sneak up on a person if they aren't prepared, and they can turn to substances for comfort and escape. This process is often gradual, so mindfulness while using substances or abstinence is advisable. If you are experiencing substance abuse, it's important to tackle those issues as part of your treatment plan with a professional. A good first step is being honest about such issues with yourself as well as professionals who are trying to help and even loved ones if you feel comfortable sharing that information. You shouldn't minimize substance abuse. Even if you can still function when you become dependent, psychologically or physically, on a substance, it is a coping mechanism that you need to change for the sake of your future.

Sleeping Too Much or Staying Awake

Sleep issues are a common side effect of PTSD, and while sometimes these issues aren't intentional, many use sleep or the lack thereof as a way of coping. Insomnia and sleeping too much can both be issues related to PTSD, and both cases can give their own kind of relief. People may avoid sleep because they don't want to have nightmares, or they may feel out of control when they sleep. They may also be unable to sleep because of panicked thoughts. Hyperarousal often stands in the way of sleep. Further, people with PTSD also have higher levels of sleep apnea. Others yet may have trouble staying asleep. Meanwhile, sleeping too long can help people cope because being unconscious longer may mean having less time awake having to deal with their PTSD. Thus, there are many ways that PTSD can impact sleep, and there are also several ways that it can be used as an unhealthy coping mechanism. Though, making sleep a priority and doing your best to get as much as you need is one of the healthiest coping mechanisms!

When you aren't sleeping well, your body's rhythms are off, which can make you more prone to stress and make you less resilient to your symptoms. Simple steps like having a sleep schedule, sleeping in a dark, distraction-free room, and being mindful of your technology use before bed can help you relax and sleep more easily. Further, medical and psychological interventions may also help. Getting your sleep is vital to your well-being, and while it's not always easy, you should take steps to deal with sleep issues.

Eating Issues

PTSD can also influence food issues, such as eating disorders. PTSD and eating disorders are common comorbid conditions. People who have experienced sexual trauma, especially sexual abuse in childhood, are more prone to have eating disorders. Those with PTSD are three times as prone to getting eating disorders as those who do not have it (L. Strickler, 2013). In 2007, Timothy Brewerton discovered how high the rates of eating disorders were within people with eating disorders. Bulimia Nervosa, characterized by binge eating and purging, had the highest rate at up to 44%. Anorexia Nervosa, characterized by self-starvation, also had a significant 16% rate, and Binge Eating Disorder, characterized by binge eating without purging, had a 24% rate. People with eating disorders may eat in excess, or they may under-eat intentionally to manipulate their unwanted, hurtful feelings. This coping method allows people to maintain beliefs that limit their progress.

Seeking psychological help and nutritional help can be good first steps for people who have both PTSD and eating issues. Further, challenging the notions that feed into the eating issues is vital because those thoughts are often related to self-image, and self-image is often impacted by trauma, especially trauma like a sexual assault that can be dehumanizing and is heavily stigmatized.

Catastrophizing

When they are dealing with hardship, people tend to catastrophize. What this means is that they tend to think the worst, regardless of the logical likelihood of the worst happening. This tendency is a common cognitive distortion (a thought that doesn't align with what is true and is based on extremes or exaggeration) that people with PTSD face. A person who has been sexually assaulted, for example, may go on a date and worry that they will experience another assault. There's always the potential that such a thing could happen; nevertheless, these kinds of thoughts reflect the person's fear and not the most common scenario. By fixating on what can go wrong, it's easy to start self-sabotaging. Using the date example, imagine that you're on a date, but all you can think about is the worst-case scenario. You're distracted, and your date senses that distraction. What could have been a meaningful connection never goes anywhere because you are focused on your worries. It's okay to be afraid, but when you catastrophize, you can't escape that fear, and it can prevent you from doing the things that you most want to do.

Being more aware of your catastrophic thoughts is one easy way to start challenging the "sky is falling" mentality. It makes sense that you would expect the worst. Your brain has learned that the worst is something that *can* happen, but expecting the worst is draining, so rewrite your dialogue. Challenge how real your assumptions are. Ask yourself if you're reacting based on present factors or past trauma. Try to see if you can poke holes in your catastrophic thoughts. Be the devil's advocate! The more you can focus on what is occurring presently and how you feel presently, the easier it will be to challenge thoughts that are being heavily influenced by the past.

Negative Self-Talk

The way you talk to yourself does impact your mental health, and when you have PTSD, you may also have shame and guilt that make it hard for you to talk to yourself in a loving way. You may blame yourself for the bad things that have happened to you, and you bring this blame onto yourself because it's easier than confronting forces that you had no control over. Negative self-talk can help you shield how you are really feeling by attacking yourself. You focus on your own faults rather than your trauma, and that's how negative self-talk becomes such a toxic coping mechanism. It can be hard to speak to yourself with kindness, but tearing yourself down creates more conflict in your mind, and it also discourages you from getting better. The best way to combat negative self-talk is being positive, but more on that later.

Self-Isolation

When you are suffering, you may find yourself pushing away your loved ones or retreating into yourself. Isolation may make you feel worse, and you might start to think that you have to suffer all alone. When you can make connections with other people, you'll feel a lot better. You don't need to let a lot of people in, but you do need a support system of some sort.

Getting Angry at Loved Ones or Yourself

You may lose your temper with people you're close to, or you may become angry with yourself as a way of dealing with your pain. It's easy to take out your feelings on others or yourself, and often, the feeling that you put out, such as anger, covers up what you are really feeling. Maybe a mother recently lost a child in a tragic accident. Then, another child may cross a busy street without looking, and the mother immediately feels a surge of emotions as she thinks of losing another child. Her heart is beating fast, and fear settles in, but she tried to push away those feelings because they are too complex. She might yell at her child, and she comes off as being angry when really what she is feeling is fear. The emotions you express aren't always the ones at the core of your emotions, and acknowledging that can help you get more in touch with your true emotions.

Self-Harming Behaviors

Self-harm is another unfortunate coping tool that some people with PTSD face, and it is an issue that is often shrouded with shame. People may turn to behaviors like cutting or burning themselves to process the emotions they have and relieve their emotional pain temporarily. These kinds of behaviors are especially common among people who have experienced physical or sexual abuse. It's also more common among young people.

Avoiding Your Problems

People with PTSD often want to avoid their problems. They want to go back to normal without having to think anymore about their trauma. They want to forget and move on, but they can't because they're not fully confronting their issues. You have to confront your problems because that's how you heal. Start by confronting little things and then work your way up to more pressing issues.

Anything that Tears Your Down

Ultimately, if anything is destructive to you rather than constructive, it's probably not a good coping mechanism. Destructive forces will always ruin your chances of improvement, so cut them out of your life.

Healthy Coping Mechanisms

When you start to apply healthy coping mechanisms, you can reduce some of the PTSD symptoms that you have and generally have a more fulfilling life. Healthy coping mechanisms make you more resilient to stress and future trauma. They help you feel self-assured, and they allow you to build yourself up rather than tearing yourself down. Healthy coping mechanisms are tools that don't just give fleeting relief. They help you heal, and they lead you to growth. The mechanisms you use may change over time, but it's always important to have a toolbox of healthy coping mechanisms at your disposal.

Re-write Negative Self Talk

Negative self-talk is one of the most harmful coping mechanisms. When you use self-defacing talk, you become more negative in general, and that negativity erodes your ability to feel self-assured and have faith in the world. Studies have long shown the power of positivity. John Hopkins has researched the impact of positivity on your health. People who are positive have less risk of heart disease. This study shows that positivity is powerful, not just for your physical health but your mental health as well.

Seek Out a Loved One

Instead of isolating, try to seek a loved one out. Talk to them about your issues, or talk to them about things unrelated to your issues, depending on what you need at that moment. A support system will make all the difference.

Find a Constructive Hobby

Hobbies are a great way to build yourself up and channel any excess energy into something productive. Re-imagine old hobbies or find new ones. Making stuff with your hobby can be extra rewarding because it feels constructive. Learn to bake and decorate cakes, make models, fix your car up, or start to knit. There are so many options, so find one that feels cathartic, relaxing, and doesn't feel like a chore.

Use Your Senses to Soothe You

Sensory experiences can be hard for people with PTSD. Certain sensory experiences can be triggering to people with PTSD, and it's important to be mindful of what those triggers are, but it's also important to find sensory stimuli that soothe you. If there are certain smells that you love, turn to those smells. Music that calms you is also a good idea. Treat yourself to the food you really love. Wear soft clothes. Look at something beautiful. Each sense has the ability to help you cope if you let it.

Set Aside Time for Relaxation

If you aren't setting aside time for relaxation, you're bound to become stressed and prone to increased symptoms. Taking special time each day when you can just relax gives you the reprieve you need to collect your thoughts and breathe through your stress. Whether you sit quietly, do a hobby, or meditate, you need to do something that doesn't feel forced and doesn't feel like you have to be doing it. Relaxation is all about wanting to do something, and sometimes the best relaxation is not doing anything!

Get Creative

Creativity allows you to confront your issues in a way that feels less confrontational. Art, writing, or playing instruments are all good options for getting creative, but they aren't the only options. We all need creative outlets, and even if you don't consider yourself a particularly creative person, letting your imagination work can help you produce better ideas and do more of the things that make you happy. Creativity lets you create a blissful state of mind, and it's not something you have to take too seriously. Just have fun; that's the best thing creativity teaches you.

Find a Way to Express Pent-up Emotions

No matter what emotions you have, you need to express them. Keeping them bottled up doesn't help anyone. You don't have to tell people about how you feel if you don't want, though that's one way to let out emotions; you do need to find some method that lets you release those feelings.

Confront Your Feelings

You cannot run away from yourself. When you start to have feelings, pushing them away is a bad way of coping because bad feelings never really go away when they're not confronted; all they do is take residence in the back of your brain. They'll nag at you, even if that nagging is done until you do something about them. Addressing hard feelings can be terrifying, but it is a vital part of learning to cope. Your feelings are messy and hard to understand, but the more you confront them, the clearer they will become.

Make New Habits

For every bad habit, you want to get rid of, find a new one to replace that habit. Bad habits can ruin your life, just as good habits can transform your life for the better. It's hard to change bad habits by simply eliminating them, but if you can replace bad habits with better ones, you'll see more progress, and you'll feel less discouraged. Curate your habits carefully, and remain vigilant so that no new bad habits sneak in without you noticing them.

Go Outside

The great outdoors is known to be good for mental health, and that has long been suggested in research. The University of California Berkley has done research to support not just is nature good for people overall, but it can have specific impacts on people with PTSD. The university studied the impact of nature activities on both teens and veterans. They found that the awe of nature was healing. After rafting, PTSD patients had a twenty-nine percent decrease in their symptoms, and their stress was also significantly decreased in general. The participants had an eight percent increase in total happiness! Another study by Poulson et al. supported UC Berkley's results, and they found that veterans who visited natural settings improved their symptoms. Thus, the research widely supports taking a step into nature when you're struggling to cope. Various activities outdoors can be healing, so choose something that appeals to you. Even a quick nature walk each week can make a difference in how you feel overall.

Seek Your Higher Power

Many religious people turn to their higher power during hard times. Finding a connection with your higher power can help you remind yourself that there's something bigger than you. There are overarching forces that you are part of. You are not alone, and you have a purpose in that higher power. No matter what religion you are, or even if you aren't religious, there's some kind of higher power you can turn to. While you certainly can have a religious higher power, your higher power doesn't need to be religious. Your higher power is whatever in your life that is greater than you that drives you to be better. Maybe your higher power is parenthood, or maybe you love nature, and your higher power is nature. Whatever it is, turn that force when you're struggling to cope. Pray, go to church, bake your kids cookies, or take a walk in nature. Act in ways that remind you that there's more to life than just your trauma.

Do Something Special

Make time for special events in your life. Sometimes, you need to take the time to treat yourself to things that you wouldn't normally have. While this behavior can seem indulgent, it is a form of self-care, and it marks your own well-being as something important. You deserve to do things that excite you and that can remind you of all the wonders that the Earth has to offer. Plus, these kinds of special moments are the perfect opportunities to connect with other people. Bring your friends or loved ones with you. Special moments are ones that help you be present. Break the routine and challenge yourself to stay involved in life rather than watching it pass you by. If you don't make time to relax during recovery, you'll get stressed out and burned out!

CHAPTER 5

WHAT IS POST-TRAUMATIC GROWTH?

Now that we have a basic awareness of trauma and how it impacts both your mind and body, the next logical question is, what happens next? How do you deal with the trauma that you have healthily and productively? The answer is in learning about post-traumatic growth, a process that often happens naturally, but it is also a process that you can start to promote right now with just a few simple steps that will put you on the road towards recovery. Whatever you are feeling now, you can feel better, and you can learn to be the best version of yourself!

Getting Stuck in Trauma

As was discussed in the previous chapters, the impact of trauma can linger – sometimes for years. Essentially the brain and the nervous system can get "stuck" as the trauma remains unresolved. Some common feelings are panicking and feeling frozen by fear. While this feeling of anxiety is normal during a Fight/Flight response, it can become debilitating when you experience it constantly – even when there is no actual threat at the moment.

Some people never overcome their trauma, and that isn't a reflection of them. Trauma becomes a trap, and when trauma lingers for so long, you may start to think that it is impossible for your trauma to change. In many cases, you heal naturally and heal more promptly with interventions, but for some people, that healing never happens. Nevertheless, healing is the usual course, and when you put in a concentrated effort to heal, you'll start to see that even if your trauma doesn't disappear, you can still start to heal, learn to move beyond your trauma, and be better for your efforts.

When you deal with trauma for a prolonged time, you become tired. If you're exhausted because of your trauma, you are not alone. Trauma takes a lot out of your brain and your body, so dealing with that trauma on a daily basis makes you feel tired, even when you are properly sleeping and eating healthy foods. Thus, the only way to get rid of that feeling of exhaustion is to combat your trauma. Unfortunately, fighting that trauma takes energy that is hard to come by, which adds an extra level of struggle to overcoming trauma, and many people may be resistant to exert their energy unless they know something will work.

Trauma often causes more mental health issues. Trauma is commonly linked to PTSD, but it can also influence or cause other mental health issues. For example, it's common for people with trauma to use substances to cope, which is why trauma and substance abuse are so linked. Further, depression and anxiety are also common among people who have experienced trauma. These issues can demotivate you even more. They can make you scared and convince you that change isn't possible. Thus, you need to address these mental health issues as part of your trauma recovery process and recognize how they keep you stuck with your trauma!

Those who get stuck in their trauma miss opportunities that could make them better because they are so focused on the negative impacts of trauma. They often have mindsets that encourage staying traumatized rather than learning to grow. This mindset is normal because it's your brain trying to protect you, but as soon as you are aware that you have this mindset, you can start to change it. Once you challenge the thoughts that keep you from finding post-traumatic growth, you'll be on a new road towards recovery. You will discover that your potential growth is so much more than you have ever realized.

Negative thinking, depression, and a sense of hopelessness can also manifest. You may think to yourself, "I will feel this way forever," or "nothing helps. Despite doing your best, every day can become difficult to cope with. It's easy to get caught up in the mindset that you are stuck in your trauma and that it is a negative part of you that you have to learn to deal with while never benefiting from it. Change is a challenge, so most people default to the mindset they are in the habit of having, and this mindset can cause unhappiness and a greater fear of change. The more stuck you become, the harder it is to believe that you can do better, so it's time to make changes right now.

Trauma can start to feel like your whole personality, so it transforms your relationship with yourself. It may worsen your self-esteem and make you less confident. The things you enjoy may become unimportant because of your trauma. You become less prominent as bad feelings swirl in your brain. Trauma so easily because of the center of your life. It is the thing that rules your everyday behaviors, and it convinces you that you are broken. You start to worry that you will never be happy, and all the parts of you outside of your trauma are numbed out by the trauma. Your trauma does not define who you are.

Your trauma makes you feel less connected to yourself, but it also makes you feel less connected to the world around you, which is a burden. You may feel like you are outside yourself and you are looking into your life. Trauma can worsen your relationship with other people, and you won't always have the energy to commit as much attention to your relationships as you would like. You become focused on yourself, and when you only focus on yourself, you become disconnected from the world and the interconnectivity that is so vital in human behaviors and well being.

Don't become complacent about your trauma. Complacency makes you reluctant to follow up on change. Being complacent is tempting because it requires less of the emotional burden that comes with recovery. You may want to take your recovery easily and only give a half effort, but you have to throw yourself into this process. Commit to getting better because, without any commitment, you're bound to get stuck, which is highly discouraging. When you start to feel better, you may back off on the heavy work of trauma and think you're in the clear, but you need to keep pushing to see the full results of this process.

There are few things that feel worse than being stuck. However, people who have undergone trauma can do more than survive that trauma. They can actually experience "Post Traumatic Growth." It should make you feel enthusiastic that you can be better than ever. Trauma doesn't have to become a permanent hardship, and you need to remember that you are so much more than your trauma. It's time to learn to focus on the things outside your trauma and take back your life! You can be better than ever with post-traumatic growth, and that's something to be hopeful about!

Post-traumatic Growth

In the mid-1990s, psychologists Richard Tedeschi and Lawrence Calhoun of the University of North Carolina, Charlotte, developed the concept of post-traumatic growth, which is still an area of extensive interest, and research about this growth continues to develop. Post-traumatic growth (PTG) is learning to do better and come out ahead after one has experienced trauma (Tedeschi & Calhoun, 1995, 2004). Adversity doesn't have to cripple a person, and it can actually motivate them to do even better and function at a greater level than they ever did before, which is the most promising idea of PTG.

Essentially, one does not just survive, but one can go on to thrive. While sometimes survival is all you can manage, you deserve to do better, and you should take the opportunity to strive for more. They don't bounce back from challenges; they bounce forward. Getting through the day is not the same as using that day to do better and advance yourself. Trauma makes you feel awful, but it can still be great fuel for you to learn and grow.

It is important to note that PTG is not the same as resilience. Resilience describes people returning to their previous levels of functioning. Meanwhile, PTG spurs positive change and higher functioning. With PTG, it is not just a return to baseline- but a profound change in how one perceives themselves and the world. PTG represents the healthy shifts in your life that come from the recovery process, which requires you to rethink your core beliefs, challenge the narratives you've created about your life, reinterpret your goals, and utilize new perspectives and norms because the old ones were interrupted by the trauma (Tedeschi et al., 2018).

Tedeschi and Calhoun suggest that PTG tends to occur in five general areas:

1. Embracing fresh opportunities in your life
2. Creating personal strength
3. Learning to have gratitude for your life
4. Forging relationships with others
5. Becoming more spiritually developed

These five areas allow you to take a holistic approach rather than focusing on just one part of your life. By dealing with these five areas, you manage the far-reaching impacts of trauma and how that trauma can influence so many parts of your life. As you go through this process, you may realize that your trauma is impacting your life in ways that you don't realize. Often, people don't see the full impact of their trauma until they start to unpack that trauma and evaluate the ways it changes their behaviors.

Up to one in seven trauma survivors report experiencing beneficial changes in some area of their life, according to the predominant research in the field (Linley & Joseph, 2004).

Tedeschi & Calhoun often use the metaphor of an earthquake to describe the process of PTG. The seismic impact of an earthquake shatters everything – and does the experience of trauma. A traumatic makes the sufferer doubt their perception of the world, and it challenges them to think in new ways about that perception. The through the process of PTG, therefore, allows people to challenge areas that held them back before, and they can start to fix issues that limited them and look at things with fresh eyes. If these perceptions are not challenges, the PTG cannot be accomplished (Tedeschi & Calhoun, 2004).

Although post-traumatic growth often happens naturally, without psychotherapy or other formal intervention, it can be facilitated. The next chapters will explain how. They will also teach you the ways in which you can add therapy and other more formal treatments to balance your recovery process. Why wait and hope that post-traumatic growth will happen when you can take your future into your own hands and encourage the growth that will make you better than ever. You don't need to suffer anymore, and you don't have to believe that you can't use your trauma to do better. Post-traumatic growth is a scientifically backed process that helps you process and overcome your trauma in exciting albeit scary ways.

Why Post-Traumatic Growth?

Post-traumatic growth allows you to do more than just recover from your trauma. Rather, it allows you to grow through your trauma. Some people stop at resilience but don't you want more than resilience. Wouldn't it be nice to use your trauma constructively? Fortunately, as many as ninety percent of trauma survivors have had at least one benefit from post-traumatic growth. Thus, PTG is an obtainable goal that most people will be able to reach if they invest time and effort into this recovery journey.

Post-traumatic growth is a mental shift. It changes the way you look at your trauma and your future. This process requires an open mind, and you must accept that growth can come through pain. When you open your mind to the potential you can reach, you feel happier, and you start to see that you are not doomed to live with your trauma forever. Positive outcomes are not only possible, but they are expected in this process.

PTSD can make you feel hopeless, but there is hope that not only can you get your life back, but you can turn it into something more. Stress can motivate you. While some stress is harmful, there are types of stress that actually make you work harder and more efficiently. It encourages you to work harder and push through the discomfort you feel. When you have stress, you know that you have to act and keep going. While it's possible, post-traumatic growth requires awareness and a concentrated effort, so it encourages you to be more mindful and maintain awareness of your feelings.

Post-traumatic growth recognizes how important your trauma is to you and your development. Your trauma is a huge part of your life, and PTG teaches you that it doesn't have to be that big. You can focus on the better future you want. No one wants to have trauma, and nothing can take away the pain that trauma causes, but you can learn to be better for it.

Important Notes About Post-Traumatic Growth

It's vital to get rid of any misconceptions about post-traumatic growth because it's not just about getting rid of trauma. With PTG, you have to start adding more positive facets into your life, using theories supported by positive psychology.

Post-traumatic growth doesn't mean forgetting. It doesn't mean ignoring what happened or never thinking about it again. Trauma doesn't disappear. Bad situations will always be part of you, but you can learn to live with those parts of you, and they don't have to throb painfully each day.

Post-traumatic growth is not magic. You can't snap your fingers and be better. There's no easy solution to trauma or PTSD, but this method is straightforward. It still takes time and effort, but the objectives are clear, and the path is hopeful. While it is straightforward, post-traumatic growth doesn't come easily, so be ready to work!

You will still have hardships going forward. When you go on this journey, you have to have faith in the process, or you can become a self-fulfilling prophecy. When things get hard, you must remember to keep going. Some days will be easier than others, and that's normal. Ups and downs are part of getting better, and your trauma influences how long it takes to get better.

The deeper the trauma, the more work you'll probably have to put in. Trauma that has long been under-addressed takes time to work through because you have to be aware of the trauma before you get rid of it.

This method doesn't work for everyone, no method does, but it is widely effective, so give it a try even if you are skeptical. These steps are well-known coping tools that are applied in various therapeutic styles as well as in alternative medicine and meditation practices. You cannot erase trauma, but you can learn to work through that trauma and use what that trauma has taught you to advance yourself. That's the beauty of post-traumatic growth; you get to better than ever, so you're not just getting back to where you were before your trauma. You are taking your trauma and using it as fuel to be your best self.

CHAPTER 6

FACILITATING POST-TRAUMATIC GROWTH

Somatic Therapies

T he body is the key to the mind. You first have to calm the body's response to trauma, shifting it from danger/alert to relaxed/controlled. Only then can you begin to recognize and process the mental and emotional aspects of the trauma. When you incorporate your bodily processes in your recovery process, you have a more holistic recovery style that allows you to have the eventual post-traumatic growth that you want!

Psychotherapists are frequently trained in areas like Somatic Experiencing™, Sensorimotor Psychotherapy, or the Hakomi Method, which can all be useful for people with PTSD. The methods in these types of therapy vary, but these approaches all deal with the body to help people recover from trauma. They suggest that the body should be a valuable tool in the recovery process.

Somatic Experiencing

Somatic Experiencing™ is just one style of somatic therapy, and it focuses on how trauma can wreak havoc on a person's nervous system, and with such an impact on the nervous system, the person may not be able to deal with the trauma, and the nervous system will make it harder for them to recover. Thus, by helping the patient become more aware of these processes, they can start to deal with the experiences that they were unable to process. The painful feelings can become a thing of the past.

When people use this kind of therapy, they start to become in touch with their bodies. They learn tools they can use when they have physical tension, and when they let go of physical tension, they can also let go of emotional tension. With this process, patients learn to hone in on certain sensations, how to use exercise to their advantage, breathing techniques, and how to ground themselves when they feel anxious. This therapy helps patients create new patterns that allow them to think in new ways and respond more helpfully.

When you are in this type of treatment, you may not actually talk a whole lot about the trauma itself. Rather, you will deal with the sensations related to that trauma, and you may be asked to recall what you presently feel about past incidents. The core assumption of this treatment is that your body doesn't forget the trauma you have experienced. Your body clutches onto the trauma, and then the trauma is part of your conditioning, which means that it can dictate your fight or flight response. Thus, you can have physical and mental issues related to these responses that your body has in place to try to keep you safe.

Sensorimotor Psychotherapy

Sensorimotor Psychotherapy™ is a treatment that focuses on your relationship you're your body. Created by Pat Ogden, this technique uses your body as the main tool for dealing with your trauma. Sensorimotor Psychotherapy does not neglect your cognitive behaviors, but it insists that those behaviors can be changed by using your body as a starting point. This treatment uses psychotherapy and somatic therapist to find the best parts of each treatment approach. This approach helps people create connections with their body and mind as a way of healing their trauma. People trained in this treatment guide patients to go through their trauma again in a place that is safe. They then break down the responses of your five senses and use that information to treat you.

This therapy suggests that you have all that you need to heal within yourself, and you just need to learn to self-regulate and reconnect your body with your mind. As you start to accomplish that goal, you'll be able to find more balance and get back to doing all the things that you'd love to do again.

Sensorimotor psychology follows a three-phase process:

1. **Symptom reduction and stabilization**, which breaks down the main issues that you have between your brain and body connection

2. **Processing traumatic memories**, which helps you reevaluate your responses in hard scenarios and work towards dealing with the memories that shape your reactions

3. **Reintegration**, which helps you start to utilize the new connections between your body and mind that you have made. You learn several techniques that help you maintain connectivity and healing.

Hakomi Method

The Hakomi Method of Experiential Psychotherapy is another approach that focuses on your bodily experiences and how your body relates to your trauma. This method was created by Ron Kurtz, who wanted to use some experimental treatment options in conjunction with more normalized somatic techniques. This theory suggests that, by looking through your body into yourself, you can promote transformation and start to grow. What this means is that you can use your body to understand unconscious processes and bring them into consciousness. When you become aware of such things, you can start to shift your behaviors and form a healthier connection between your mind and body.

While using Western ideals, this method also incorporates Eastern methods like Taoism and Buddhism, so it adds mindfulness practices, empathetic exercise, and the idea of a loving presence. This process also includes several other methods that incorporate the body, such as:

➤ Reichian breathwork
➤ Bioenergetic analysis
➤ Feldenkrais method
➤ Structural bodywork
➤ Eriksonian hypnosis

- ➢ Neuro-linguistic programming
- ➢ Psychomotor therapy
- ➢ Gestalt therapy

The Hakomi Method can help you focus your attention and learn to manage your bodily responses caused by your PTSD. This method focuses on your ability to change your mindset through somatic awareness, which is why it can be so effective for many PTSD sufferers.

Journaling

Journaling is a well-researched method that you can do to help yourself because it allows you to be more reflective and confront some of the issues that you may be tempted to keep to yourself. When you journal, you learn to look at the world in new ways, and you have a creative outlet for your thoughts. Journaling is a habit that people overlook, but it is scientifically proven to help people with their mental health and even their physical health. No matter what your issues are, journaling is well worth the effort, and it's something you can do for just a few minutes a day!

Research widely supports journaling. Journaling for just fifteen minutes a day can improve your health, research shows, as long as you keep it up consistently for several weeks. Journaling has been found to make you less stressed. It also improves your immune system so that you have a lower risk for illness. When you're better physically, it's easier to focus on your mental health, and physical health often impacts mental health. Journaling also has been shown to improve your mood and mental health in general. Plus, it improves your memory function, which can help you overcome some of the ways that PTSD impacts your memory processes and cognitive processing. Thus, there's a long history of studies that show just how impactful one little journal can be.

Writing information down not only helps you process that information, but it allows you to see patterns. When you journal, you can start to figure out what triggers you and the habits that may be hurting your progress. You can also see what kind of behaviors result in positive outcomes. Knowing your patterns is one of the best ways to make changes because being conscious about how you tend to react shows you how to break bad habits and form better ones that encourage a PTG mindset. The more consistently you practice journaling, the more you'll start to make connections and see patterns. There's a reason why many therapists have clients use journaling in therapy! It helps you see certain issues more quickly.

When you journal, you don't have to focus on writing carefully. Don't try to write high-quality writing. It is great if your writing is high quality, but don't pressure yourself to write well. Write from your heart and express your feelings in a way that feels natural to you. You don't have to be a great writer to be a great journaler. As long as you're expressing your ideas and logging your behavioral patterns, you'll see great results. You don't even have to write when you journal. Some people prefer to use other methods like using art to show their processes rather than words. Other people may prefer to keep an audio journal. Be creative with your journal of choice and choose something that reflects your abilities and interests. You can also combine multiple methods however you desire.

While many people undermine the validity of journaling, it has been proven to be beneficial for people because it helps you bring unconscious thoughts to the forefront of your brain. You learn about yourself and your trauma. You start to see what worsens your trauma and what makes it better. Journaling allows you to heal yourself, and it gives you information that will be much harder to get through other methods. With just a few minutes each day, journaling can have lasting impacts, and even when you overcome your trauma, it can help you check in with yourself and maintain your growth trajectory.

Be Grateful

Gratitude does a lot for your mental health. Harvard University suggests that being grateful makes you happy, based on studies about positive psychology. Thus, gratitude is not only part of politeness, but it helps your mental and physical well being. Gratitude helps you see the world in a more optimistic way, and you learn that the good things in your life are stronger than your trauma. Trauma seems strong, but the truth is that it is weak compared to the good forces you have around you. All you need to do is learn to use those good forces and be grateful for their existence.

Consider the bad, but don't let the bad become the most prominent part of your life. I'm not asking you to forget the bad things that have happened to you because denying your trauma doesn't help you address it, but don't give the trauma more weight than it deserves. Instead, be glad about what you do have rather than being bitter about what you don't have. You're never going to have everything that you want, but when you make the most of the resources at your disposal, you can think in creative ways and create a situation that enables you to grow and empowers you to challenge the negative and erroneous messages that your trauma creates.

Reflect on the things that make you the happiest. When you are tempted to ruminate about the negative parts of your life, try to think about the good things that you have going on. Consider the things that bring a smile to your face and try to incorporate those things into your life more frequently. You can't always get rid of negative forces, but you can always add positive ones. Even during hard times, you can find moments of happiness. It's like when you go to a funeral: the sadness is palpable, but you can also talk about the ways that the deceased person made you happy. Multiple feelings can coexist. You don't have to be completely sad just because something sad has happened! Feelings are complex, so utilize that complexity for growth.

Take time to serve others. Doing things for other people reminds you that your life is bigger than yourself. You have a greater role in humanity, and your actions impact other people.

Seek your higher power. Your higher power is the thing that makes you feel meaningful. It is something greater than yourself, and it motivates you to be your best self. Some people think that having a higher power means you have to be religious, but that is not the case at all. Your higher power can come in many forms. It focuses on the positive forces that shape your life and make you feel like you have a greater role in the universe. For some people, a higher power is God or other spiritual entities, but for others, their higher power can be other abstract things like parenthood or nature. Be grateful for your higher power, whatever it is.

Take time to appreciate the little things. Small things like your child's smile or blooming roses can add happiness to your life. All those little things don't seem like much, but when you add them up, they are potent, and they can change the way you feel about your life. Take comfort that amid the worst moments of your life, there are always those little things. When you cannot find big things to be grateful for, it's time to double down on those subtle moments of appreciation. Don't take them for granted. Embrace the way those moments shape your life.

Show love to the people who support you. You have to be grateful for the people who help you and give you love. The people in your life are not perfect, and they may make mistakes, but as long as they are overall caring and healthy for you, you should be grateful for them. You can even be grateful for people who are not in your life anymore. Some people are not healthy for you to be around, but they still may have taught you useful lessons and given you positive things while that relationship was strong. Human connection is one of the most rewarding parts of human life, which is why learning to appreciate the people you connect with is so vital for your well being.

Use positive language. Research from John Hopkins suggests that whose family has a history of heart disease are thirteen percent less likely to have a cardiac event when they think positively. This research reinforces other studies that show that not only does positivity make you feel better, but it makes you healthier too. Positivity can improve your mental health and make you less stressed. It allows you to focus on growth and be more than resilient. You can do more than you ever imagined by changing your mindset. Stop talking badly about yourself. You may think that negative self-talk doesn't affect you, but it does. It changes the way you see yourself and the way you approach your trauma, so learn to talk about yourself more kindly.

Maintain realistic expectations. It's hard to be positive when you set your expectations too high, so remember to keep your expectations in check.

The words thank you are powerful. Never forget that. Appreciate people's good intentions and appreciate your own efforts. Write about your gratitude in your journal, end each day thinking about what you are lucky to have. By practicing gratitude daily, you change the way your mind thinks, and you will feel a whole lot better! Further, be grateful to yourself for how far you have come and how much you have fought. Gratitude is just one thing you can do to help your PTSD, but it can make a profound difference, and it is useful to you beyond just your trauma.

Mindfulness and Meditation

Research widely shows the power of both meditation and mindfulness. The research suggests that when you use these techniques, you are less stressed, and you are both physically and emotionally healthier. Meditative practices help you process your sensations, and they allow you to be more in touch with yourself.

Meditation is a practice that has you take time to be in tune with your body. It uses your mind-body connection to motivate positive change. It helps you become more focused, and it allows you to be mindful and focus on your current senses. You can use guided meditation, but you can also guide yourself through meditation. Mediation often includes breathing techniques, and in the process, you are asked to acknowledge the sensations you are experiencing without judgment or analysis. You process what is without worrying about what was or what will be.

When you meditate, it is good to create a calming environment so that you aren't interrupted and you feel tranquil. Experiment with different meditation styles to see what works the best for you. The key to meditation's effectiveness is consistency, so try to create a meditation routine.

Mindfulness can be part of meditation, but it also can be a distinct practice. You can be mindful in all areas of your life. Mindfulness is the act of being present and aware of what is happening around you. It asks you to pay attention to your senses. You can be mindful in several areas, such as you can be mindful about your hunger cues or how your body feels when you exercise. Mindfulness is about staying in touch with your mental and physical cues and using them to make harmonious decisions that promote happiness and defy trauma.

One technique that you can use in both mindfulness and meditation is visualization. Imagine what you want from your future in a vivid way. Think about how that thing makes you feel and what it would look like. Go through all five senses to imagine what you want. When you imagine what you want, it is more likely to come true because you send messages to your brain about what you want to accomplish, and your brain can then act on those things.

Mindfulness and meditation can help you process your feelings and is often a tranquil experience. These techniques will show you how to respect your senses and embrace them. They prevent you from avoiding and shoving away your sensations, and they're also incredibly calming practices.

Use Social Media Wisely

Social media can cause more harm than good if you are not careful. It is not bad to have social media, and it can be a very helpful resource for people looking to keep in touch with loved ones and make connections with like-minded people. Nevertheless, if you are not mindful of your social media use, you can feel worse about yourself, and you can trigger your trauma.

Limit your social media use. Pay attention to how much you are using social media. Everyone has limits about how much social media use is good for them, and many people go beyond that safe limit. If you're spending hours each day on social media, you may be limiting the growth activities that you're able to do in your normal life, and you might be exposing yourself to media that does more harm than good.

Curate your social media use. Don't be afraid to mute or unfollow people. Certain content may be damaging for you to see, and it's okay to limit that content and control that. Controlling your social media feed is a great tool for people with trauma, and it allows you to have a healthier social media experience.

Check-in with yourself frequently to make sure that your social media use remains healthy. Your social media use can strengthen your post-traumatic growth, but it can also make it harder for you to overcome your issues, so be aware of how social media impacts you and know your social media boundaries.

Self-Help Techniques

There are many things that you can do right now to reduce your trauma response, and there are many techniques beyond the ones that you find in the book. The methods provided are the ones that are most common and most transformative for most cases of PTSD. You can pick the methods that are applicable to your case, so don't feel pressured to do them all, but applying several of these methods is often the most effective for people who want to get better. Remember that you are in charge of your growth, so you get to define the measures you take to do that.

Hit the Books

There are many resources within this book that can get you started on your PTSD recovery journey, but there are so many additional resources online that you can use. For example., finding PTSD workbooks can help you work through your PTSD in a more structured way if you need additional guidance. Getting as much information as you can empower you to help yourself, and it shows you a wide range of ways that you can address your PTSD. Further, it makes you feel less alone and reminds you that your PTSD doesn't change your value as a human, and it doesn't mean you're weak. PTSD is a well-studied condition that science and psychology can explain.

Do Things That Give You Joy

Take some time to focus on your hobbies. Your hobbies are activities that allow you to relax. Hobbies are things that you don't do because you have to or because you think you should do them. They are recreational, and they help you use your energy in productive ways. For anyone who wants to have a fulfilled life, you have to have hobbies. Those hobbies can come in a number of forms, but make sure you have special activities that allow you to learn, build your skills, and relax can help with trauma.

Research supports that creative outlets are incredibly advantageous among people with PTSD. Start drawing or use other forms of art. You can try learning an instrument or write stories or poetry. Other creative options include photography, model building, and sewing. Whatever you choose, find something that allows you to express yourself and use your pain to create.

Use old hobbies that have historically given you joy. Now is a good time to think back on activities you used to love and give them another try. If you find that they don't give you joy anymore, move on, but the nostalgia of old activities can be appealing. Maybe you quit playing piano years ago; try picking it up again and see what happens! Or, if you used to play soccer in high school, kick the ball around. You don't have to be good at the activity or play at the level you once did, but you can still use it to have fun and relax.

Let go of activities that make you feel bad. If there are hobbies that make you feel bad about yourself, it's time to move on from them or put them on the backburner. You don't have to stick with something just because you liked it in the past or you're good at it. Make time for more joy rather than using that time to do things that you feel like you have to do.

You can also try new hobbies that you don't know much about but that interest you. Never prevent yourself from attempting new pursuits. Trying new things pushes you from your comfort zone, and it helps you expand your world. It's thrilling to try new things, and it can give your life new meaning. You don't have to do anything extreme like skydiving but learning a new skill can help you channel your energy and attention to things that help you with your PTG.

Leave time for leisure, and do things that are special. Your life shouldn't be filled with activities that feel like work. It is vital that people relax if they want to have their health. There is a wide range of hobbies and activities that can make you feel better. Find something that makes you feel better and that emphasizes your skills and wishes.

Friendship and Love

You cannot go on this journey alone. Research proves how useful a support network can be, and it suggests that people who have social support have decreased severity in their PTSD. I've already emphasized the importance of having a support system, but when you have trauma, the method of how to accomplish this can be a challenge. When you have trauma, you may be resistant to some of your relationships, and you might struggle to feel like yourself. Thus, it helps to take a few of the following steps to ensure that you use your support system to your advantage. When you worry that you're dealing with something that no one understands, it feels isolating, but at the very least, we all have hardships, and most people experience some kind of trauma in their lives. Thus, as human beings, we can connect through our hurts.

Refuse to close off your heart because of your trauma. Trauma may cause you to be fearful of relationships. You may worry about the pain that love can cause. It is true that love can result in pain, but love much more rewarding than it is harmful, and if you don't have people to love, you will not be fulfilled in ways that are deeply satisfying.

Don't isolate yourself. It may be tempting to deal with your issues alone and then reconnect with people when you have sorted through those issues, but that strategy is limiting, and you'd be much better off including people in your life.

Be honest about your feelings, and reach out to your loved ones. When you are honest about how you are doing and take the chance to share your feelings with people in your life, you will feel better about your overall situation and think again about the idea of gratitude. When you connect with other people, you become more grateful, and it's a relief to have that brightness and joy in your life that enriches your self-development. When you have feedback and care from people you love, you start to thrive.

Find a support group. Support groups are a great therapeutic option that can help you meet people who share similar issues as you. Trauma can be hard for outside people to understand, but when you find a group who has experienced similar trauma or PTSD, you feel like you belong, and you can learn more techniques to be better.

Service dogs and other service animals can be a great option for people with PTSD. Animals can be soothing for people, and service dogs are known for their skills to help you when you have PTSD symptoms. Dogs are very perceptive, and they can help relax you and keep you safe as you deal with your trauma; plus, they are loyal companions.

Create healthy boundaries in your relationships. Healthy boundaries ensure that you respect the emotional and physical boundaries of other people, but you have to enforce those boundaries with people in your life. All relationships need boundaries. For example, you may not want someone to hug you, and that is a boundary you establish with them. If they breach that boundary, you should communicate that you have that boundary, and you can explain why that is if you are so inclined. If the friend, upon knowing that you have a boundary, doesn't respect your boundary, they are not respecting you and your limits, and you will need to take further action. Boundaries give relationships some structure, and for each relationship you have, you may have different boundaries. These boundaries ensure that you feel safe in relationships, which is why they are so important, especially when you have trauma that may cause you to blur boundaries or that may be worsened by a lack of boundaries

When you reach out to other people, you start to break from the isolation that PTSD can cause. No person can grow alone. It takes relationships to feel fulfilled in life. If you are alone, your life has less meaning, and you may wonder what the point is. That doesn't mean that you cannot spend time on your own, and it doesn't mean you need a lot of relationships. It's okay to want time and space for yourself, but it is harmful to have no one in your corner. Humans do better when they have relationships, but you get to choose the kind of relationships that you want and need in your life. Part of the growth that you will experience is that your trauma can help you form connections with other people, so don't deny those connections.

Alternative Therapies

Alternative therapies can be great options for people seeking relief from PTSD. These options are not mainstream, but they do show promise in treating PTSD at least supplementally. Alternative therapies give creative solutions to people who want to help themselves, and many of them may seem a little out there, but if you see them through, you may find that they are effective for you!

One interesting technique you can use is the Emotional Freedom Technique. It is a method that people use for both emotional and physical distress. It was developed by Gary Craig, who said that negative feelings and pain are caused by disruptions in energy. This technique has been used to help with mental conditions like anxiety and PTSD. There's not a whole lot of research on it, but one study showed that it helped veterans with PTSD with their symptoms, and over half of the EFT group no longer had the symptoms required for a PTSD diagnosis. Thus, the results of the research are limited, but this alternative therapy is still young and shows some promise. This process is not unlike acupuncture in that it uses various points of the body—inspired by Chinese medicine. You tap these points to send signals to your brain and influence your stress levels.

Aromatherapy is one excellent choice that has been shown to be soothing for people with a wide range of conditions. When you use essential oils, you influence the limbic system of the brain, and the response of your brain can then reduce some of your PTSD symptoms. People with PTSD most often use the essential oils topically, through inhalation, or in baths. Be warned that smells can produce strong responses, so if you are sensitive to certain smells that may be associated with your trauma, this option may not be the best option for you, but you can try different oils and see if any work well for your needs.

Many people have good results from hypnosis. Hypnosis is a process that uses your subconscious and conscious thoughts to complete desired outcomes. It puts you into a trance-like state, and in this state, you are more open to suggestions. This does not mean that a hypnotist can make you do something that you don't want to. Hypnosis only gets people to do things that they are willing to do, and it does not allow someone to control your mind. Hypnosis is good for helping you deal with traumatic memories and some of the other symptoms related to PTSD. You can use hypnotherapy in conjunction with other therapeutic methods. Some mental health professionals will guide you through this process, but you can also find dedicated hypnotherapy scripts and videos.

Alternative therapies are often not enough on their own, and you should also consider employing traditional therapies, which you will learn about in the next chapter. Nevertheless, these practices are not dangerous, and the worst that can happen is that they don't work for you. Many people have found success with these practices, so why not give a few of them a try and see if they impact you?

Learn Your Tendencies

You need to learn what most influences your PTSD. This is one of the areas that your journaling can help you with. When you know your tendencies, you better understand your habitual reactions and emotional responses. Everyone reacts differently, and your reactions are often fueled by your past experiences and your personality. Some of your tendencies are genetically motivated, while others may be environmental. Most are a combination of multiple factors. Regardless, these tendencies are part of who you are, so learn to work with those tendencies rather than trying to erase them.

Learn your triggers. Everyone has things that trigger emotional responses. In pop culture, the word trigger is often overused and misused to apply to anything that makes us feel upset or unhappy, but a true trigger is a lot more than that. A trigger creates an emotional response, and it is motivated by whatever trauma you have. For example, a certain smell or sound can cause a person with PTSD to have a flashback because it reminds them about their trauma. That is a trigger and learning things that might trigger you can help you be prepared in situations that may be filled with triggers. Thus, you can learn to deal with the triggers rather than trying to avoid situations that may trigger you.

Note your common responses to triggers. Pay attention not only to what triggers you but how your brain responds to those triggers. Your reactions will differ based on your trauma and the triggers. You can then find new ways to mediate your responses once you understand what your responses are. You can learn to react to triggers in healthier ways that promote healing and growth rather than perpetuating your trauma. You can also inform other people of what might happen if you're triggered, which enables your support system to understand you better and support you through your trauma.

Talk to your support system about your habits and triggers. Sharing these parts of yourself with other people may seem intimidating to you, but when your support system knows what causes you distress, they can help you work through that distress, and they can be more careful about certain things like the language they use and the way they interact with you. You cannot avoid triggers, but with awareness, you can better control your circumstances, and doing so gives you time to work on your trauma in a safe space that facilitates growth.

When you know your tendencies, you start to adapt the way you respond to incidents, and it is that shift that gives you the conditions that help you grow. You can learn these tendencies with techniques like journaling and mindfulness, but a therapist or another mental health professional can also help you learn your tendency, and often having an outside source helping you can expedite the process, and that person can help you pick up on things that you may take a while to notice on your own. Therapy helps you acknowledge your behaviors and feelings, and then it shows you how to change them. Therapy can be confusing, and you may know how to get started with it, so it helps to understand some common types of therapy and who those types help.

CHAPTER 7

THERAPY FOR PTSD

The Gift of Therapy

Therapy is a great option for people who are experiencing PTSD because it allows a professional to guide them through the feelings and responses that they have. When you are dealing with PTSD, you may feel a little lost, and you may need an outside party to help you get back on track. Even with a strong support system, it can be hard for you to feel understood without a professional. Additionally, professionals can teach you coping techniques that you can use outside therapy. They can also help you condition your responses and process what has happened for you. Thus, no matter what your goals, there is likely a way that therapy can help you have post-traumatic growth.

When you go to therapy, you learn a lot. You learn about how the human brain operates generally, but most importantly, you learn how your brain works specifically. You start to uncover truths about yourself that you may have never thought of before. Therapy starts a series of changes in your life, and it allows you to learn new skills and take on a new perspective. Different types of therapy teach you different things, but there are lessons to be learned in whatever kind of therapy you choose, and as long as you make an earnest effort in your therapy, you can get something out of it.

Therapy allows you to cope with your trauma and learn techniques to maintain a healthy mindset. One of the greatest things you learn in some types of therapy is coping tools. So many people lack proper coping skills, and that lack of coping skills makes it hard for them to move past trauma. Bad coping skills will also make you less resistant to future traumas. Thus, learning to cope in ways that are constructive is vital because if you rely on destructive coping skills, you cannot grow, and you will be trapped with that stuck feeling, which can perpetuate those negative feelings that you have.

The idea of therapy can be overwhelming because there are so many types of therapy, and they can feel like a confusing alphabet soup that means very little to people who don't have much experience in therapeutic circles. Even people who are familiar with therapy may get confused about all the different types and what type would be best suited for them. Thus, it's beneficial to create a brief guide of the types of therapy and who each type of therapy may be best for. Therapy is not easy, and it feels like a hassle when you're already struggling, but it can be healing.

With so many types of therapy, there is sure to be something that suits everyone. It may take a little searching and a little guessing and checking, but in time, you can find something that best helps you create post-traumatic growth. Not everyone has the resources for therapy, and not everyone needs therapy, but if you are able, it doesn't hurt to give therapy a try. Plus, therapists best know how to personalize your treatment plan to solve your specific trauma. Thus, you can learn information about yourself and your state of mind that you cannot get anywhere else.

How to Know if Therapy Will Be Useful

You may be wondering if therapy is a good choice for you, and the blanket answer is that it probably is good for you, but there are certain scenarios that may indicate that therapy could be necessary or highly recommended. Of course, the choice is always up to you, but therapy can help you get faster results and will give you a customized plan for your recovery. Unfortunately, therapy is often stigmatized, but think of it this way: you go to a doctor to fix your hurting body, so it also makes sense to go to a professional who can help you fix your mind!

If you are worrying that you will hurt yourself or others, you should seek professional help. Trauma can cause you to act in ways that aren't normal for you, and thus, you may be in a dangerous state of mind that can cause unwitting reactions that may be harmful. You may have thoughts of suicide or self-harm, which are strong indicators that you need extra help from a professional. You can still use this book, but you should also seek the guidance of a professional who can help you work through your issues more effectively.

Therapy is also good if you suspect you may have other mental health conditions that are comorbid with your PTSD. Depression, substance abuse, and anxiety are some common issues that may occur with trauma, and you may benefit from having professional treatment in these cases. Monitor how you are feeling to judge how urgent therapy is for you.

People with C-PTSD may also need the extra help that therapy can provide. Due to its complexity and the inclusion of multiple traumas, C-PTSD can become tangled and hard to understand, and a therapist can help you untangle all the trauma that has become woven together. C-PTSD also often results from childhood trauma, and childhood trauma can often be incredibly confusing to work through. Thus, therapists can be of great use in these scenarios.

If you are overwhelmed, therapy is an ideal option. Even as you're reading this book, you may feel like you have no idea where to start and worry that you are in over your head. If you are feeling this way, a therapist can provide more structure, and they can help you understand the steps you need to take to promote growth. Some people thrive with clear parameters about what they should do next, while self-guided treatment often relies on tools and for people to use with less exact parameters. Being overwhelmed is normal, but if that feeling doesn't go away, a therapist can help you make sense of your situation.

Therapy is suitable if your trauma has taken over your life. If you feel that you are struggling to function, therapy is advisable. While trauma is painful and PTSD is often intrusive, they impact people's levels of functioning to varying degrees. Your ability to function doesn't reflect on your worth as a person. If you function less, you aren't more of a freak or less competent. All it means is that your body and brain are reacting in a different way. Nevertheless, it's still important to get the appropriate amount of care for your needs. A therapist can help you function better more quickly, and a therapist also takes some of the weight off your shoulders.

If your relationships and ability to feel joy are suffering, it may be time to seek professional help. These two signs are huge red flags that you need more help with your trauma. That level of deprivation can easily make you feel hopeless and alone. Therapists can show you how to appreciate your life and find joy even as you continue to struggle against your trauma.

Many people, even those without trauma, go to therapy because they need a third party to speak with. As supportive as loved ones can be, they are often too involved in your life, and you may want someone to talk to who is outside that personal bubble. Therapists are trained to help you without the baggage that comes with having a personal relationship with you. Your friends, for all their merits, probably don't know how to deal with trauma, and it's hard for them to keep an unbiased mindset. Therapists, meanwhile, allow you to speak more freely and without worrying that you'll ruin important relationships by bringing up hard truths.

In general, most people will benefit from therapy of some sort when they have PTSD because PTSD is such an invasive condition. Its symptoms are hard to deal with, and the underlining symptoms may require a lot of unpacking. Therapy is a great space for people to learn and grow. It creates a systematic process for recovery and increased structure that many people benefit from having.

Therapy for You

Therapy is an incredibly personal experience. Everyone experiences it from a unique perspective, and they go into it with unique needs.

Therefore, the type and intensity of your therapy will depend on what you need and want. It's important when entering therapy to understand the ways this process is personalized and how you can make the right choices for the results you want. If you don't find the right therapeutic process for you, you may not feel satisfied with your results. Plus, you need to remember that just because one process works for someone you know doesn't mean that the same process will work for you! We're all different, so no approach appeals to us all, and the many options for therapy reflect those differences.

Before you do anything else, I want you to remember that going to therapy doesn't make you weak. Many people seem to think that only weak people go to therapy, and they assume that if you're going to therapy, you must be "crazy." However, therapy is a classroom of sorts, and it teaches you skills that allow you to cope and grow. It's also a space that allows you to express your feelings without the fear of retribution. It is confidential, and for many people, it is life-changing. People go to therapy for healing, but it doesn't mean that they are inherently wrong or weak. It takes strength to invest in yourself and confront your issues, so people who go to therapy are actually incredibly strong and smart.

Finding the right therapist may take some time and multiple appointments, but it is an important step. Make sure that you find a therapist who specializes in trauma. You can make an in-person appointment with your therapist, but online therapy and teletherapy options have expanded your ability to get care, especially in rural areas where access to certain therapeutic types may be limited. You have to find a therapist who you like. If you don't like a therapist, don't be afraid to mix things up and get a new therapist if one doesn't work for you. Try different types of therapy. Therapy is like finding the perfect pair of jeans: you have to experiment with the size and cut to see what most flatters you! This process may seem tedious, but when you find a treatment plan that works for you, you'll be excited for what the future holds.

Be persistent with your therapy. If you do not keep up with your therapy, or if you refuse to do your assignments, there's no way you're going to make the progress you want. You may move forward, but you'll be dragging your feet. Make the most out of your therapy because there's no point in taking that time from your day if you aren't going to use it to the fullest. Therapy may scare you, but that fear shows that you are doing something to confront your trauma, and that's a good sign.

Always be upfront with your therapist. Lying or misleading your therapist won't go well for you. You need to be vulnerable in therapy and show a willingness to go along with the treatment. While even when you hold stuff back, therapy can still have some benefits, you will get the most out of your time if you are honest with your treatment provider or team. Just as you should be honest about symptoms and concerns with a medical doctor, you should also be this way with someone who is helping you heal your mind. Don't just be honest about your trauma, but also be honest about what you want your therapist to do and raise any concerns you have as therapy continues.

If it isn't working, it isn't your fault. Therapy is tricky, and it might not always work the way you hoped. While it is one of the most scientifically backed methods to cure your PTSD, nothing is a sure thing. At the very least, therapy will give you coping tools, and you can use those in all areas of your life. When you don't respond to therapy, consider that you might've chosen an unideal therapy type, or your therapist might not be right for you. Therefore, don't give up right away. Further, remember that it sometimes takes weeks or months for people to see results in therapy, so hang in there!

Use supplemental techniques to assist your therapy. This book is full of supplemental techniques that you can use to enhance the therapeutic process. Any of the tools given here are great in conjunction with therapy, and many of these methods are commonly recommended by therapists to their patients. Further, you can use non-traditional methods, such as acupuncture, to add to your experience. Your treatment plan doesn't need to entail just one prominent fix. Find habits that work for you and that are harmonious when you put them together. As you do that, you'll have the best results that you can have.

You may also want therapy to help with relationships that your symptoms may have damaged. For example, you may be suffering marital issues or other mental health issues because of your PTSD. Those issues are things that you also need to address during this process if you want to free yourself from your trauma. When you have PTSD, there may be several areas of your life that need healing, and it's great to confront any issues that you have because confronting those issues gives you the clarity to focus on your growth!

Therapy comes with a lot of choices, and one of the biggest choices that you'll make is what kind of therapy you want to do. There are many types of therapy, and there are even more than the ones listed in this book, but included are some of the types of therapy that are most common and most effective for people who have PTSD or trauma. Thus, you should find something that appeals to you within these types, and once you understand what each one does, you can begin to evaluate what you want to try and what would best address your set of problems and symptoms.

Cognitive Behavioral Therapy (CBT)

What Is It?

This type of therapy is perhaps the therapeutic gold standard, which has long shown results in a wide range of conditions. Cognitive Behavioral Therapy (CBT) is one of the most common therapies available. This therapy style focuses on your cognitive patterns and how to change them. This means that this psychotherapy treatment helps you notice and adjust thought patterns that cause negative thoughts and responses. Thus, it can help people process the thoughts that feed their trauma responses. This therapy posits that you have automatic thoughts that shape your behaviors and feelings, and when these automatic processes are negative, your actions become fueled by information that isn't necessarily reflective of the true situation.

There are many types of CBT, including Rational Emotive Behavioral Therapy (REBT), Dialectical Behavioral Therapy (DBT), and Multimodal therapy. Each of these types of therapy has its own techniques and focus, but they all use the same basic cognitive rewiring. Some are more applicable to certain conditions. For example, DBT was developed for Borderline Personality Disorder. You'll learn more about cognitive therapies, like Mindfulness-Based

Cognitive Therapy, later in this book, but don't worry too much about the individual therapies just yet.

Common Techniques

This therapy teaches you to identify when you are having negative automatic thoughts that cause unideal behaviors. It also shows you new skills that help you deal with triggers and engage with real-life scenarios that may cause you trouble. In this therapy, you also learn to solve problems because issues often stem from triggers, and learning to manage those triggers helps you get control over your life. Another important part of this therapy is learning to set goals for yourself because creating goals allows you to plan ahead and teaches you to shape future outcomes; it also gives you direction. CBT also helps you learn to be mindful of your patterns, and this awareness can guide you and allow you to both monitor your behaviors and track your progress. It also helps you notice how you feel as you are triggered or have episodes. This therapy tackles cognitive distortions, and those cognitive distortions often cause overreactions because of overgeneralization or catastrophizing that is spurred on by the trauma.

Who Benefits from It?

Many people benefit from CBT, especially if they have negative thought patterns that feed into their symptoms. For example, if you think your traumatic experience is your fault, that can trigger a thought pattern that results in maladaptive behavior. If you have co-occurring conditions like an eating disorder, depression, or anxiety, CBT can be especially helpful. It can help you address the fears you have and learn to think more positively. It is a strongly recommended treatment for PTSD by the American Psychological Association. It is also a versatile treatment that can help a wide range of people. There are also many practitioners who use this method, and that availability can make it a convenient choice for people who may struggle to find professionals in their area.

Things to Note

There has been good research supporting the effectiveness of this therapy because CBT is such a common type of therapy. It is one of the most widely studied therapies, and it is useful because it has a relatively short turnaround time. For some issues, just a few sessions can help people change, but for issues like PTSD, it will probably take around twelve to sixteen sessions. Sessions can be done individually, but group CBT is also an applicable method. Other therapies may not be as efficient and may require more money and time resources than CBT.

Eye Movement Desensitization and Reprocessing (EMDR)

What Is It?

One of the best choices for people with PTSD is EDMR. Eye Movement Desensitization and Reprocessing Therapy is a fantastic choice for people with trauma because it was specifically designed to help people lessen the impact of trauma. Thus, it is an effective treatment for trauma. During this therapy, patients are asked to relive their traumatic moments so that they can remember them and then process those memories. As they process the memories, the patients are able to lessen the impact that those memories have on their daily lives. This therapy uses eye motions to control the attention of the patients and help prevent memories from overwhelming them. The eye motions help patients focus, and diverting someone's attention makes painful thoughts less powerful.

Common Techniques

This therapy has eight phases that are spread over around a dozen or so sessions. The first phase eases patients into the treatment and begins with an evaluation that allows the therapist to create an appropriate treatment plan that considers the trauma and needs of the patient. Once a patient has completed the initial phase, a therapist will teach exercises that facilitate the patient to cope with the memories they are going to address. Then, the therapist manages specific memories to target, and they determine what sensory processes to include. The next four stages of the process employ the EMDR and begin to target the memories. The therapist guides you through the eye movements, but don't be alarmed if other movements are part of the process. Your therapist then guides you to think about your feelings and the memories you have. Throughout the process, the therapist remains mindful and will help you if you get overly distressed. In the final phase, you and your therapist will evaluate your process. This technique sounds complex, but it is not as scary as it sounds!

Who Benefits from It?

Many people who are struggling to deal with traumatic memories can benefit from EMDR because it is made for people with trauma and PTSD. While this therapy may not be as effective for other mental illnesses, it is one of the best options for people with PTSD. If you have other comorbid conditions that need to be taken care of, you may benefit more from other types of therapy; however, limited research does show that it can help people with other conditions well. Anyone with trauma can work through their trauma using this method, and it is a fairly efficient method for both short-term and long-term development.

Things to Note

This treatment has been customized for trauma survivors, but that doesn't mean it is the best option for all people. Like CBT, this therapy doesn't take too many sessions. Often, it is completed in twelve sessions, but some variance may occur. Many resources, including the Department of Veterans Affairs, recommend this practice strongly for patients with PTSD, and several studies suggest that it helps short-term and long-term outcomes for people with traumatic stress. This therapy is definitely one you should consider because of its specific links to trauma treatment, and it is highly specialized for people like you.

Acceptance and Commitment Therapy (ACT)

What Is It?

This type of therapy blends several types of therapy to have unique results. Acceptance and Commitment Therapy (ACT) uses traditional therapy methods in conjunction with cognitive therapy methods to help people continue their lives and move forward from the emotions that hold them back. It allows people to better understand how their emotions and avoidance techniques influence their well-being. It helps people accept their situations and then commit to their acceptance through their actions. People naturally want to have more positive feelings and fewer painful ones, so we often try to ignore what hurts, but avoidance doesn't solve our issues! Negative emotions are normal, and ACT teaches people how to manage those emotions and move on from them. Further, it helps them respond to those feelings in more positive ways and discourages maladaptive coping. A foundational idea of this treatment is that when we suffer, it is because we try to avoid hard feelings. Thus, it suggests that your symptoms will improve when you start to accept your traumatic memories and learn to process the feelings associated with those memories.

Common Techniques

There are five goals that dictate the treatment style of ACT. The first goal is commonly called "creative hopelessness" by professionals, and it relates to acceptance; it asks you to acknowledge that you will never be able to deal with painful emotions through avoidance. ACT also suggests that your issues are caused by your attempts at controlling your pain through things like avoidance, but to control it, you start to focus only on trying to keep the bad emotions away while ignoring positive feelings. The third tenet of this therapy is recognizing that you are not your thoughts. After you have a traumatic experience, you may think that you are a flawed, broken person, but while you feel such is the case, that doesn't make it the truth. Thus, you need to challenge your thoughts and question if they are true or if they are a product of your emotions. The fourth lesson of ACT is that you need to halt any attempts to control your emotions. Instead, you must be open to the feelings you have. Finally, you must commit to action, which means that you must evaluate your values, the things that make your life feel meaningful, and commit to activities that reflect those values. You must make that commitment, even if it means facing the uncomfortable feelings that you've tried to avoid.

Who Benefits from It?

ACT can help people with a wide range of mental health conditions, including PTSD because it helps people deal with feelings related to a traumatic event. For people who experience substance abuse or other self-destructive tendencies, it can be especially helpful because it helps those people learn that temporary relief is not a long-term solution to pain and shows them how to use other methods to cope. People who like to avoid their feelings can benefit highly from this therapy style, and people who like taking action will also relate to this style because it is an action-based therapy. This therapy, using its five goals, teaches that by facing your pain, you can live a full life.

Things to Note

ACT can be an easily accessible option, but it is not as mainstream as some options like CBT, which may be concerning to some people. You can find worksheets and information online and on apps. You can also attend ACT workshops, seek teletherapy, or go to a traditional therapy session. Thus, the options to get this treatment are extensive and can make getting this treatment pretty straightforward. Different options may appeal to people who have odd schedules or want less formal options. This therapy is not one of the most studied options, but it is getting more popular in the psychological community.

Emotionally Focused Therapy (EFT)

What Is It?

Some therapies focus more on the individual than the social network of that individual, but Emotionally Focused Therapy (EFT) is a therapeutic practice that emphasizes bonding and attachment in adult relationships. It helps people create trust in relationships and ensures that you have a secure bond with loved ones. It often deals with couples or families who are struggling to have secure relationships. Secure relationships are marked by each person feeling safe in the relationship and not fearing abandonment, rejection, or other hurts. People who group up with unreliable caregiving, such as children who grew up in institutional care or abuse and neglect victims, may not have formed secure attachments with their parents. Those insecure attachments can then cause prolonged relationship worries into adulthood. People may become avoidant, anxious, or a combination of avoidant and anxious in their relationships rather than feeling safe. Past trauma can fuel insecure attachments, but EFT can help reduce any relationship worries that consume you.

Common Techniques

EFT teaches you to express your emotions in healthier ways. It allows you to communicate and understand how your past trauma and emotions influence your current emotions. It often helps you realize feelings that you might not have recognized previously. Further, it teaches you how to bond with people and feel secure in your relationships. You learn how to interact in new ways, so if your trauma influences how you talk to loved ones, these techniques can be very useful.

Who Benefits from It?

This therapy is not for all people with PTSD because of its focus on relationships. This therapy could be useful for adults who have trauma-related childhood experiences that influence their ability to form secure bonds in adulthood. This practice is mostly related to trauma that influences your relationships with other people. This therapy also helps you communicate better with your loved ones because it teaches you to create a connection with rather than detachment from people in your life. It also helps you understand how you may ignore past emotions because of current emotional issues that hide those other issues. This therapy also helps you listen to your loved ones better, so you can respond to emotional situations better.

Things to Note

If you want to try this therapy style, be sure to find a therapist who is specifically certified in EFT. The certification is given by the International Centre for Excellence in Emotionally Focused Therapy. This therapy style is not as common as some of the others, so it may be harder to find a therapist who suits your needs and makes you comfortable. Your options are more limited, but teletherapy and online options may give you more flexibility for this type of therapy.

Group Therapy

What Is It?

Group therapy is what the name implies. It is finding a therapist-led support group. In these groups, you sit with people who relate to what you are going through, and rather than having an individual session, you have a session with people who share your issues. Group therapy reminds you that you are not the only person in the world with trauma, and when you join a group, you start to realize that other people have had trauma that is similar to yours, even though it's never exactly the same. People in groups commonly share the same kinds of feelings and concerns, which makes you feel less alone. You feel understood in a good group, and that can be comforting for people whose trauma makes them feel alienated or misunderstood.

Common Techniques

Group therapy is effective for various reasons. First, it lets you learn from others. While learning coping strategies from your therapist is helpful, a group can give you better insight into what works for other people in your position. Further, you can learn from the mistakes in the group as much as you can learn from the successes. Group therapy helps you form a support system that knows what you are going through. Additionally, your experiences benefit other people's improvement as well. You end up with a whole community of people who share their feelings and ideas. You learn to express yourself and have an outlet for your struggles. Group therapy prioritizes shared learning, and depending on the group, the professional in charge may employ various therapy styles. Thus, group therapy can be a diverse experience, and the exact methods of the sessions depend on what kind of group it is.

Who Benefits from It?

Group therapy is a cost-effective option that is great for people who feel alone when it comes to their trauma or who feel misunderstood. This method is a great way to form connections and meet peers in a safe space. Group therapy is not always the ideal choice because you get less individual attention, and as a result, you may not get to discuss certain deeper issues that may influence your well being. You may also be limited in how much you can say. Certain topics and comments may be off-limits to ensure that everyone feels safe within the group.

Things to Note

You can use group therapy in addition to other therapy, but you can also use it on its own, and it is a cost-effective option for many people. Not all groups are led by a therapist, so be sure to research what kind of group you are attending and who is in charge. Group therapy options in your area may be limited, so if you don't find a group that you like, you may have to seek other options. If you cannot find a group you like, online mental health forums combined with individual therapy may provide a good balance between social healing and managing your issues through a professional.

Exposure Therapy

What Is It?

This type of therapy helps people who are fearful and can't seem to confront those fears. Thus, Exposure therapy is a therapeutic method that helps you face the things that scare you. When you have trauma, you may try to avoid certain things because they bring up hard-to-handle feelings. As a result, you limit yourself, and you may avoid doing things that you would like to do but avoid due to your anxiety. For example, you may love listening to live music, but because of trauma, you may avoid crowded venues and concerts. You get in the habit of avoiding what worries you rather than facing it, and that tendency often makes you more fearful, and it can become debilitating. Your trauma starts to rule your life! Exposure therapy addresses these issues by exposing you to the things that make you afraid. It's easier to manage your fears in this therapy because you are in a safe environment.

Common Techniques

Therapists gradually expose you to the things that worry you. If you were terrified of dogs, for example, the therapist might start by showing you pictures of dogs, and then they may eventually progress to have you do things like being in the same room as a dog or pet a dog. Through exposure, people become less anxious, and they expand the things they can do and the situations they can be in. There are several types of exposure. The first type is direct exposure, called in vivo exposure, which will have someone doing an activity that embodies what they are afraid of. Imaginal exposure helps people imagine whatever they are afraid of, and people with PTSD may be asked to think about traumatic events. Some therapists may use virtual reality in cases when real-life exposure wouldn't be practical or controllable. Interoceptive exposure has people focus on certain sensations that may be troubling to that person. Therapists will each create different plans for clients that fit the clients' worries.

Who Benefits from It?

Exposure therapy is good for anyone who struggles with fears of certain places, situations, things, or activities. Those with specific phobias, anxiety, OCD, and PTSD all can benefit from this therapy when fear makes it hard to do certain things. This therapy helps people reduce and eventually stop their avoidance of certain things, and it helps them confront feelings that they might not be able to confront on their own.

Things to Note

Research shows that exposure therapy is effective for people with PTSD, and this practice continues to grow. Technology expands the capabilities of people who are using these techniques. This therapy is often scary for patients because it forces them to face the things that most intimidate them, but it is safe and perfectly applicable to trauma. There is also Written Exposure Therapy (WET), which is a five-session process that is more cost-effective, and participants are less likely to quit WET than other exposure methods; it includes thirty-minute writing sessions that help people write about their trauma. Prolonged Exposure Therapy, meanwhile, takes up to fifteen sessions and more gradually exposes patients to the things they fear, and it includes homework assignments.

Cognitive Processing Therapy (CPT)

What Is It?

This therapy will have familiar components. Cognitive Processing Therapy (CPT) falls under the umbrella of CBT, and it is known for helping people who have gone through traumatic events. Like CBT, it helps the patient learn what their negative beliefs are, and then it helps them reframe their thoughts, which are commonly fueled by trauma. It also helps patients process the events that caused their trauma, and by processing that trauma, they can start to rewrite the thought processes that reinforce PTSD. This therapy allows you to use cognitive methods and writing to deal with your trauma.

Common Techniques

This method uses many of the same methods as CBT, but it focuses on automatic thoughts in the context of how those thoughts influence a person's PTSD. In the early moments of this therapy, therapists have patients write an impact statement about their trauma and how that trauma affects their lives, and how it frames their view of the world. The patient then must start the processing process. AS they process, they write details of their trauma. Their therapist uses the Socratic method, along with other techniques, to ask the patient questions that help patients challenge their thought processes. Finally, the patient starts to use new strategies that utilize the new beliefs they have learned. They handle several areas related to the trauma. Some of the areas that this therapy targets are: self-esteem, safety, control, intimacy, and trust, which are common issues for people with PTSD. These issue areas often cause anger, fear, guilt, and other negative feelings that can cause you to act out and lose control over your life.

Who Benefits from It?

This therapy has been found to be useful for people who have experienced a wide range of trauma. Some of the commonly cited examples include veterans, rape and abuse survivors, and survivors of natural disasters. This method is one of the methods that the American Psychological Association strongly recommends for people who are experiencing PTSD. It is only recommended for people who have gotten a PTSD diagnosis as it specifically focuses on PTSD. Further, if you struggle with reading or writing, it might not be the best option for you because of the extensive written homework, so you may be better off with options such as Prolonged Exposure Therapy. People who may be exposed to more trauma, such as first responders or people in the military, may find this therapy especially useful.

Things to Note

CPT is generally administered over twelve sessions, and while it often has the written statement, in some cases, that step in the process will be excluded, so various therapists will alter their methods slightly. Further, you can see this type of therapy both in individual and group settings, so that gives you some more treatment options, which may be appealing. Providers may have specific certification for this kind of therapy, but there are also treatment manuals that practitioners can use to help them give this kind of therapy if they'd like it but cannot find a provider who has a lot of experience in this type of therapy.

Positive Psychology

What Is It?

Positive psychology is a technique that can be applied in various therapeutic styles. It was founded by Martin Seligman, who created the ideas that led to the theory of learned helplessness, and he noticed the power of positivity; he posited that psychological practitioners paid too much attention to negative components, which led to the creation of positive psychology in 2000. Mihaly Csikszentmihalyi helped Seligman with his initial positive psychology paper. Since that time, there have been thousands of studies exploring this idea and supporting the positive approach to therapy.

Positive psychology is defined by its focus on the positive parts of human life rather than the trauma and pain. It doesn't ignore the hardship, but it helps people to see their strengths rather than making them focus on their weaknesses. It helps people acknowledge feelings like joy, love, and happiness. It relies on gratitude and kindness. It also helps people apply positive principles that encourage good behavior rather than discourage bad behavior. This technique is used in a wide range of situations like workplaces, coaching, relationships, and teaching, so you can widely apply it to whatever issues you have and is incredibly useful.

Common Techniques

This type of psychology is known for its optimism because it relies on changing your mindset to change your life. It helps people look at the parts of their lives that give them happiness. Instead of fixating on your trauma, you learn to think about what fills you with good feelings. You learn compassion and self-compassion techniques. You also improve your self-esteem and overall outlook on life. This therapy helps you see life through a new lens, and many people who learn to be more positive are more successful, and they feel like their lives are more meaningful. This method teaches people to set goals, and it teaches them how to experience positive feelings. It has clients reflect on their strong areas and shows them how to use those strengths in their lives. It also guides the client to find the silver linings in situations.

This method used the acronym PERMA:

- ➤ **P**ositive Emotions—learning to enjoy yourself and feel good about your life
- ➤ **E**ngagement— becoming engaged in activities and invested in them
- ➤ **R**elationships— forming positive connections that help you grow
- ➤ **M**eaning—finding something bigger than yourself that gives your life meaning
- ➤ **A**chievement— a drive to do better and accomplish your goals

These techniques are useful because you can measure them and see how well you are doing, and they are clear objectives you need to reach.

Who Benefits from It?

This practice can be great for people who find themselves feeling hopeless or depressed. If you're tired of feeling pain, this therapy can show you the brightness of life and start to become more positive. The concept of this technique is simple: you need to switch the way you think. By reframing your life and view of the world, you can transform how you think. People often don't realize the things that bring them happiness and confuse what leads to happiness, so positive psychology can help people who may be a little confused about the meaning of happiness. Most people can benefit from more positivity, and for those who have experienced trauma, this therapy can teach you to be more grateful for the good things in your life. It shows you that there's more to life than your trauma and that you can choose to prioritize the good feelings and the strengths of your life.

Things to Note

This technique is one of the newer styles, so there is less outstanding research on the subject. Nevertheless, research has widely shown that positive thinking can be transformative. Many people underestimate the power of your mindset, but based on research, this method can be effective. Though, some people may need to confront some of their issues before they are ready for this kind of method. This technique has measurable goals and parameters that make it easy for you to track your progress and see how far you have come.

Mindfulness-Based Cognitive Therapy (MBCT)

What Is It?

This type of therapy is a take on a classic therapy style! Accordingly, Mindfulness-Based Cognitive Therapy (MBCT) is a type of treatment that a trio of therapists created—John Teasdale, Zindel Segal, and Mark Williams. They incorporated techniques from Jon Kabat-Zinn into their therapeutic practices. MBCT is a therapy that combines cognitive therapy (a highly effective therapy that focuses on your thought patterns and how they related to feelings and behavior) combined with mindfulness techniques. Mindfulness refers to being present and aware of current senses, which can help people with

PTSD, who often experience flashbacks and may get stuck with their thoughts in the past.

Common Techniques

This therapy will use basic cognitive therapy techniques, which help you understand how your thought patterns work and how to correct those thought patterns, but it deals with these cognitive ideas through the lens of mindfulness. Therapists teach clients to be mindful using several exercises. One of the most common exercises is mindfulness meditation, the act of gaining awareness of the body through breathing techniques. This approach to treatment is often heavily physical, so it's not just sitting around talking and has many action exercises.

This therapy may also incorporate other mindfulness exercises, such as grounding, which helps calm clients by reminding them of their surroundings (such as asking them to focus on certain items in the room). This practice may involve stretching or even yoga to facilitate a connection between your mind and body. It also may include things like body scanning, which has clients focus on various parts of their bodies. Breathing techniques and awareness are often prioritized in this type of therapy.

Who Benefits from It?

This treatment was originally made to help people who have depression, so if you have depression that is comorbid with your PTSD, this is a fantastic choice. This type of therapy has since been found to help people with other conditions as well. The mindfulness exercise helps people with high-stress levels, which can be excellent for those with PTSD. Because it is a cognitive practice, it teaches you how to replace negative thoughts with more helpful ones so that your brain responds in new ways. This therapy also maintains the idea that you are prone to falling back on old patterns, so it encourages you to carry on the methods provided even once you stop sessions.

Things to Note

Most of the research on this therapy has been focused on its treatment of depression. This therapy has shown immense results in people with depression, and it helps people get through depression while also reducing their risk of relapse. The specific applications of this treatment for PTSD are less studied, but there have been some promising results among patients with PTSD (Roychowdhury, 2017). Further, other research shows the effectiveness of CBT for PTSD, so because MBCT is a type of cognitive therapy, it is likely quite effective. Like other cognitive practices, a lot of the work will be done outside of therapy sessions, and you will have homework to complete. Thus, much of the work will be done independently, but this type of therapy usually takes effect quickly.

Psychadelic-Assisted Therapy

What Is It?

Psychadelic-Assisted Therapy is a therapy that used psychedelic drugs to help people with the therapeutic process, and these drugs are used in a highly controlled setting. Psychedelics alter the way you think, and they frequently cause you to be more open and expand your mind. Many people experience spiritual endeavors when they use this drug. They may feel more creative and open to various ideas. This therapy has long-held curiosity, and it was revived in the 1990s after a period of dormancy. The therapy continues to grow. Though the research is still limited, so there are a lot of questions that many people have about the usefulness and long-term results of this practice.

Common Techniques

This method uses a variety of drugs to have a different effect on people. The method combines the controlled drug use with traditional therapeutic methods. This practice is still budding and forming, so the techniques vary, and therapists may use different techniques based on your needs and their clinical experience.

Who Benefits from It?

This technique has been found to be good for chronic PTSD and other mental health conditions, and it is safe when applied in a therapeutic setting by a knowledgeable professional. This therapy is riskier and less proven than many of the other methods, so it may not be the best option for many people. Many people may be uncomfortable with drug use, even in a clinical setting, because these drugs do change your brain and the way you think. These methods are growing, but there are still a lot of questions that surround them, so be mindful of this fact.

Things to Note

There are several substances that may be used in psychology. MDMA is a drug that has the potential use for PTSD. Some other drugs that could have psychological impacts include ketamine, LSD, psilocybin, mescaline, ayahuasca. You should always make sure to find a therapist who is experienced in this field, and the application of this kind of therapy differs based on laws and regulations where you live. Many people use micro-dosing on their own for therapeutic results, but it can be done in a clinical setting which makes it safer. The research on micro-dosing is not strong or well-developed, but some research shows that it may make people more positive and can help in therapeutic outcomes. Nevertheless, you still need to use some traditional therapeutic means to get any benefit from this therapy.

Disclaimer

Psychadelic-Assisted Therapy requires a professional guiding the therapy, and you should not try to administer any of the drugs mentioned here without any assistance. Some psychedelics can cause negative symptoms that could do you more harm than good, which is why they should be taken in a controlled environment and with caution. These therapies have been shown to be safe but only in highly regulated environments. People handle drugs differently, so taking them unsupervised can cause trouble. Psychedelics can be dangerous, and they can cause things like health issues and hallucinations, so keep that in mind. Outside a medical setting, many of these substances are illegal.

CHAPTER 8

PHYSICAL WAY TO ASSIST IN TRAUMA HEALING

The Power of Your Body

Your body allows you to do everything that you love to do. While the mental work will take up the bulk of your journey to growth, you cannot deny the way your body plays a role. Your body allows you to do everything that you want to do, and it is the thing that allows you to act. Otherwise, you would only be able to think and not do. Use your body as a tool. Some trauma may cause people to resent their bodies, but it helps to embrace your body. Learn to love your body flaws included, but if you cannot love your body right now, start by feeling neutral about your body. You might not love every part of your body, but you can still respect it for the things that it can do. Remember that the joy of your body refers to what your body can do, not what your body looks like. Your body has aches, pains, and limits, but it keeps going, and it is surviving, and that's pretty cool. Your body can do so much, and it should be part of your recovery process.

Get Your Beauty Sleep

Sleep is one of the most important things that you can do for yourself. When you sleep, your body repairs itself, and your brain processes memories and things that have happened to you. Thus, sleep promotes vital functions, so without it, you're going to struggle to act efficiently and do what you need to do to grow.

Research shows that people who sleep more and have a better sleep are healthier. The Sleep Foundation explains how PTSD can cause sleep issues, but sleep issues also contribute to PTSD symptoms, so when you aren't getting your sleep, you may have a range of complex sleep-related issues. Research shows that people who have nightmares and sleep issues before going to war had higher rates of PTSD, and then the sleep issues can worsen symptoms, and the fatigue makes it harder to resist the effects of PTSD. Thus, not having sleep can be a nightmarish situation.

Take some steps to improve your ability to get to sleep, stay asleep, and get good quality sleep. Put your phone away before bed. The light from your phone can make it harder for you to sleep. Create a distraction-free sleep environment. That means that you should make sure that pets aren't in the room to wake you up. Limit outside sounds as much as you can, and use things like eye masks and blackout curtains to limit the amount of light in the room. Ensure that the environment is comfortable—nice sheets, not too cold or hot, and good air circulation.

Have a bedtime routine and sleep schedule. When you have a routine, your body's natural rhythms will help you fall asleep and wake up naturally. This routine helps you get better sleep, and it allows you to get the amount of sleep you need. It may be tempting to stay up late and spend time playing games or reading, but that option is not ideal because it messes up your sleep, and it interferes with your natural rhythm, which is especially important if you suffer from insomnia or sleep issues related to your trauma.

Exercise can actually help you with sleep. Working out has a lot of perks, and research suggests that when people exercise, they sleep more and also have better quality sleep. While exercise may not be what you want to do when you're exhausted, it can help you have more energy in the long run.

Sleep helps you function better, and your body needs it, so while it may be hard to get to sleep and stay asleep, you should do everything you can to get your beauty sleep because sleep does impact your overall health and your ability to deal with trauma.

Breathing Techniques

Using breathing techniques is a great way to get your PTSD symptoms under control, and these techniques are good for your mental health in general. PTSD management doesn't get much simpler than this. These techniques are easy to learn, and they don't take a lot of time. Thus, even if you are skeptical about them, they are well worth the try, and the research on the matter supports that deep breathing helps you reduce stress, which can then decrease your PTSD symptoms. Further, when you feel your symptoms start to get worse, you can use this breathing to calm down and work through triggers.

One of the most effective methods is diaphragmatic breathing. Many people take shallow breaths, and they don't use their diaphragm when they breathe. As a result, they may take short breaths, and these breaths can make you more anxious, stressed, and send you into a panic. Diaphragmatic breathing includes using your diaphragm, an abdominal muscle. To breathe this way, you want to start by being in a comfortable position. Place your feet flat on the floor, and relax your shoulders. If you need to focus, you can close your eyes. Place a hand on your chest and the other on your stomach. Take a few breaths, and if your abdomen is rising and falling as you breathe, you are breathing the right way. If it isn't, ensure that it is, and continue to take deep breaths as you feel your stomach rise and fall. Maintain this practice until you feel calmer.

You can also try breathing-based meditation. Research by Seppala et al. shows that breathing-based meditations are an effective PTSD treatment among veterans. They used Sudarshan Kriya yoga to see if breathing-based meditation influenced PTSD outcomes. The research focused on the experiences of veterans, but the effects could certainly be similar in other PTSD sufferers. These kinds of meditation guide you to focus on your breaths and use that as the central principle of meditation. By adding these types of meditation into your routine, you may be able to reduce your PTSD symptoms. These techniques are great because you combine the positive impacts of both deep breaths and meditation.

Using breathing methods can help you manage the stress that makes your PTSD worse, and it can give you the techniques that you need to calm yourself. When you don't breathe properly, your body starts to feel anxious, and your stress levels rise. Then, you feel like you're in danger, and your PTSD may start to send you into overdrive. Thus, by taking some time each day to focus on your breathing, you can become more mentally clear, which will allow you to do things that help you grow. Learning to breathe in a satisfying manner may take some time and practice, so keep at it, and don't become discouraged if it takes a while to get in the habit of breathing better.

Nutrition

Food gives you vital nutrients, and several studies have linked positive eating habits to positive PTSD outcomes, just as unbalanced eating habits can cause worsened PTSD. Your diet impacts how your brain can work, which means that if you aren't getting the nutrients you need that you can very easily sabotage your progress and worsen your symptoms. It may be hard to balance your diet because your PTSD can ruin your appetite, or you might use food to numb the negative feelings you have. Still, you should have a well-balanced diet. Include a wide variety of foods, and choose foods like whole grains, fruits, and vegetables. Don't avoid good groups unless you cannot medically have those foods. Thus, you should include healthy fats, carbs, and proteins so that your energy levels and body functions are strong. Ensure that you are eating nutrient-dense foods. Fruits, vegetables, and whole grains are packed full of good things. Finally, treat yourself every once in a while because food should enjoyable, and it's okay to have things that aren't necessarily nutritional but give you joy!

Movement and Exercise

Getting your body moving is a great way to help your PTSD. This movement can be whatever you want it to be, but the point is to avoid dormancy and employ more activity. Keeping your body moving helps your brain and your physical health. It can also be a great stress reliever.

People with PTSD may struggle to find the motivation to exercise, and a racing heart from exercise can worsen hyperarousal and some of your other symptoms. Nevertheless, exercise has been linked to better overall health and improved mental health. Thus, while you may not have much motivation to exercise, it can have long-term impacts on your mental wellbeing. One study of people with PTSD showed that light exercise, such as walking or resistance training caused a huge drop in the participants' symptoms. Thus, while cardio and activities that get your heart rate up may induce symptoms, certain types of exercise may make you feel better.

Be consistent with your exercise. Find a routine for your exercise, and throughout the week, you'll want to do a few different activities to work different muscles and parts of your body. Mix techniques like stretching and weight lifting to challenge yourself and keep your body in shape.

Start to take walks or engage in other nature activities. These activities aren't too strenuous, and they can make you feel connected to the outside world. Doing activities outside the gym can make them feel recreation more than something you have to do. Don't look at exercise as a chore. Instead, use movement that makes you feels good. If it doesn't make you feel good, try other options that make you feel better.

You don't have to work out a lot, but exercise is good for your mood, and it makes your body strong and resilient. Exercise can be something as informal as dancing in your kitchen to your favorite song or walking your dog, so don't be afraid to be creative with the techniques you use!

Staying in Tune with Your Body

Always listen to what your body is telling you. Your body knows what you need, and it sends you signs to keep you updated on how it is doing. Pay attention to these signs and take them to heart. For example, when your stomach rumbles, you probably feel hunger. Listen to that hunger and all the other sensations that give you vital information about how you are. When you are aware of your body, you are more mindful of your mental processes as well. You can notice the signs of traumatic responses before they creep up on you— Check in with how you are feeling physically because that feeling can often match how you are doing mentally. Your body and brain are connected, so never forget how important that link is. It's time to start using that link to your advantage!

CHAPTER 9

LIVING A LIFE OF POST-TRAUMATIC GROWTH

I f you want to have long-term results from this journey, there are several things that you have to remember. These things will help you survive and push forward when you have rough days and difficulties. By keeping these things in mind, you can resist future trauma and keep up the fight against the trauma you have. It's easy to begin a post-traumatic growth journey, but maintaining that journey is a challenge for many people who become tempted to give up or slow down. Keep going! It's for your benefit to do so.

Know What to Expect

If you don't have the right expectations, you're going to go astray. That's the bottom line of post-traumatic growth. So many people go into this process, not realizing the nuances of it. You have to realize that there is potential for failure. You may not see the results that you want, but more likely than not, you will. Most importantly, the results hinge on your commitment to the process and the work you are willing to put in. As I've said, this process is not magic, and if you expect that trauma will vanish with a snap of your fingers, you've come to the wrong place!

Expect for it to get worse before it gets better. This is news that people don't like to hear, but it's an important warning for anyone trying to grow. Growth starts with hard labor. It's like gardening. When you plant a garden, before you even have the plant in the ground, you have to till the land and do some digging. Growth takes preparation! When you are confronting your trauma, you're going to have to deal with thoughts that you've probably been avoiding. Therefore, you're probably going to feel pretty bad at some points during this process. You have to learn to accept what has happened to you, and that can be pretty tough when you likely don't want to think about those hardships. Nevertheless, thinking about those hardships is what you need to do so that you can process them and move on.

Expect that recovery won't be linear. As nice as it would be to keep getting consistently better, that's not how recovery works, and if you expect that it will happen like that, you'll get discouraged. Some days may be great, while others make you feel like you are going backward. Human experiences have ups and downs, and these ups and downs aren't things that you should be afraid of because they are natural and normal. Sometimes, you'll take two steps back, and that doesn't mean you've done anything wrong. Keep going, and in the long term, you'll come out ahead, and you'll start to have fewer bad days. The bad days you do have will become more manageable.

Expect that sometimes other people won't understand. When people are supportive, it feels wonderful. You're in a great position if you have a support system that understands what you're going through and can be empathetic to your efforts, but the truth is that many people won't understand your trauma response. You can give them resources and try to explain to them how you feel, but people you love aren't always going to approach your trauma in a way that makes you feel better. Welcome other people's support, but know that well-intentioned loved ones don't always do the right thing. They might not mean to hurt us, but sometimes, they do. Don't take other people's actions as a sign that you should back down. Stay true to your commitment to getting better.

Expect that you don't always have to be your best. Society often pressures us to be our best selves all the time, but if we were always our best selves, the word best would lose its meaning. You can only be your best self sometimes. Some days, you won't have the energy to do as much work towards growth, and that's okay. Trying too hard to be the best all the time often leads to burnout, so it's better that you push yourself while still taking recovery at your own pace. This is your journey, which means that you decide how much you can give to the process, and you don't have to pressure yourself. The more pressure you put on yourself, the harder it is to get results. Be more organic in your approach.

Expect that some things will work and some things won't. All the methods in this book aren't going to apply to you. There will be things that you like to do and then there will be activities that don't really suit you. That's perfectly fine. The goal of this book is not to provide you a checklist of how to grow from your trauma; rather, it is meant to give you a toolbox of various tools that you can use as they apply. You wouldn't use a hammer to screw in a screw, so remain aware that not every tool works for every problem. You might not know what the tools do at first, but experiment with them. See what works and what doesn't. Testing these options is the best way to get success.

Expect to be exhausted. By the end of this process, you're going to feel tired. Recovering from trauma means that you're doing the normal things that you do in your life, but you are also heaping on a lot more activities. It's a challenge to add more to your life. We're all busy people. Thus, this process will make you tired, both physically and emotionally. In the end, you'll be able to do more, and you'll be more efficient, but it takes exhaustion to get there. It is like going to the gym. When you start running on the treadmill, it may take you eleven minutes to run a mile, but if you keep going, you can get that down to ten and then nine and then eight. At first, you feel utterly depleted after your mile, but as you keep going, that mile gets easier. You have to train your mind, which takes time.

Expect to be liberated. The good news is that your work is going to help you liberate yourself from your trauma. Many of the expectations you have are warnings about the struggles you'll go through, but the freedom you will have in the end is the expectation that is going to carry you through all that tumult. What is liberation? Well, that's up to you, but it is all the things you'd like to do but haven't done because of your trauma. It is clearing your head of clutter and allowing that space to be open for things that give you future joy. Past pain is burdensome, but when you get that out, you'll be free.

When you go into this process with the right expectations, you'll never be disappointed with the results. These expectations shape how you go into this process, so by keeping them in mind, you can prevent some of the doubts and apprehensions that await you. This journey is going to be long and bumpy, but in the end, you will find growth, and that's the most rewarding expectation of all.

Trauma Doesn't Just Go Away

Trauma is an injury, which means that you can't wish it away, and you also can't force it to heal. You can nurture it, but you can't change it. Many people think that to deal with their trauma, they have to make it go away. They have to pack it up and push it to a dark corner in their brains. Anyone who has an attic full of dusty artifacts knows that when things are packed away, they don't stop nagging at you. You open the door of the attic to get Halloween decorations, and you find yourself wading through heaps of junk that overwhelms you. Likewise, the good memories and the bad ones coexist in your brain, and the bad ones have a way of appearing when you least expect it. Thus, you've got to unpack your trauma.

You may always have a scar. Scars are the lingering marks from things that have happened to us in the past. Many of them fade over time, and sometimes, we can barely see them, but we know they're there. There's no point in denying that scars exist, but the pain eventually stops as our bodies do what they do best and heal. Your body wants to move on. It is wired to heal and fix what is broken. It has limits, and it cannot fix everything without a lingering mark, but reminders of what was don't have to be painful every time you see it. Using the tools in this book, you'll learn to confront your trauma without always feeling intense pain.

Respect your trauma even as you let it go. Don't demean or dismiss your trauma. It's vital that you acknowledge the role your trauma has in your life. If you try to deny it, you are essentially pushing it back into the musty room in your brain. To let go of trauma, you need to appreciate it for what it is. You don't have to be happy that it happened to you, but you do need to respect that it is part of your story, and it is part of your mindset. Your trauma is part of you, so if you cannot respect your trauma, you cannot respect yourself either.

Take pride in your trauma. Again, you don't have to be proud of the bad that has been done to you, but take pride in the way that you have endured despite that trauma. It's amazing that you've gotten this far and that you are making an effort to overcome your trauma. You should be proud that darkness has been part of your life without destroying you because as long as you keep fighting, there's still light shining.

Find trauma's silver lining. Find the ways that trauma has made you a better person. Even if you haven't gotten to the post-traumatic growth phase, your trauma has been an influence on who you are and how you behave. Perhaps, it has made you more empathetic. Maybe it has taught you to be less harsh. There are so many lessons that trauma can teach, and part of post-traumatic growth is learning to appreciate those lessons rather than focusing on the negative elements of trauma. Of course, I don't want to simplify things or diminish the pain of trauma, but even if it's just a sliver, there is a silver lining to trauma.

Your trauma likely represents some of the darkest moments of your life, but there is a light that can come from that moment or moments. You get to define your future. The past will never go away, but the future is fluid. It's open to change and hope. Plus, you can change how you think about the past. You can focus on good memories instead of bad ones. You can learn to coexist with the hard memories because those memories are just one part of who you are overall. What you choose to do is always more important than what happens to you because you choose what you do while you don't always choose what happens to you. Thus, focus on who you are and how trauma plays a role in your development and belief system.

Don't Give Up

When things get hard, you have to learn not to quit. The moments when you want to quit are the most transformative in your journey. There will be times when you'll wonder what the point is. You'll think that your efforts are never going to pay off. The journey will feel tiring and lonely, and you'll start to think that you were crazy for thinking that it will work. When you lose faith in the process, that's when it becomes harder to make progress because you start to back off on your commitments, thinking that they aren't going to work, so why put the effort in. Thus, you must remind yourself that giving up gets you nowhere.

The moments that make you want to quit are the moments that you are closest to change. It is in the moments that things are the hardest that mark the precipice between getting better and reverting to old ways. Self-improvement is scary because it challenges the status quo. It forces you to walk into unknown territory, and your brain will scream at you to stop because, for its survival, it has learned that it's better to stick with what it knows and to choose what comes the easiest. The path of least resistance is tempting because it feels safe, but often, that safety marks surviving rather than thriving.

Find things that motivate you to keep going and clutch onto those things. When things get hard, you need to remember what it is you are fighting for. Do you want to be able to watch a firework show with your kids? Do you want to stop feeling so angry all the time? What is it that your trauma has taken away? Remind yourself of why you want to fight instead of cowering each time you start to have doubts. You will be stronger as you take on this mentality, and over time, this thought process will become more automatic. By habitually resisting your doubts, you find the courage to keep going.

When you are struggling, remember your worst moment and remind yourself that if you don't keep going, you could end up feeling like that again. It's too easy to backslide when you're having a bad day. Many people find themselves falling further into a slump as bad things happen. You start to think, "I should quit." More than you think to keep going. Push through those feelings by reminding yourself that you don't want to get worse. You're trying to get better, which means that you can't afford to give up. A little discomfort is necessary to pull yourself from the pits of your trauma.

It's okay if some days you don't accomplish as much as you hope. Goals are important, and you want to create goals so you have an idea of how much you can accomplish in a certain amount of time, but it helps to remember that goals are flexible. If you don't reach a goal in the time that you hoped you would, push back the date and use that to plan accordingly. Goals don't have to be rigid. They need some structure, or they don't keep you accountable, but you can't predict everything that will happen, so goals don't always go according to plan. Be merciful with yourself and keep going when you feel like you're failing.

When you confront your issues, you may get scared and want to give up. That feeling says that you're on the right track. Doubt pops up when you're starting to venture into new territory. Thus, progress inherently comes with doubt. Doubt isn't a bad thing. It's not some monster creeping into your life to derail your progress. Always listen to your doubts because doubt is a survival tool, but listening to your doubt doesn't mean giving in to it. Judge what your doubt is trying to say and evaluate whether it is genuine or fear-driven.

Be Kind To Yourself

Kindness is one of the most powerful things you can do in life. Most people are great at extending kindness to other people, but they fail to extend that same kindness to themselves. Unfortunately, self-compassion may be even harder when you are dealing with trauma. You may blame yourself for your pain, or you may belittle yourself for being so trapped in your trauma. These attitudes make it harder for you to create the progress you want because they maintain a negative and disempowering mindset. Accordingly, adding self-kindness will transform your ability to complete the tasks in this book. Your kindness will spread to all areas of your life.

Look in the mirror and find things to love about yourself each day. This task may feel stupid or corny, but it helps you be appreciative of all the good things that you have to offer. Don't just look at your physical qualities, but you should also look deeper and think about the unseeable good qualities you have. What do you like about your personality? What good traits do you have? Find at least one good thing about yourself and continue to add to that list. If you can't like yourself, you're never going to be kind to yourself.

Think about what you can do rather than what you can't do. Lingering on all the things that you cannot do is disheartening, and it doesn't speak to your strength and goodness as a human being. Maybe you're not the best at art. Who cares? Your good at other things, so think about those and start to place your worth in what you can do. We all have limits. We can push those limits, but no one can do everything, so accept that you can and build up your skills rather than wasting time thinking about the skills or tendencies that you don't have. Value the potential you do have, not the potential you wish you had.

Don't bully yourself. People love to call themselves names and tell themselves that they are useless. Don't do that. Bullying often comes from a place of insecurity, and that insecurity is often related to your trauma; it provokes trauma, or it worsens the trauma you already have. Some trauma may also cause insecurities. Self-bullying validates the insecurities you have, but what you want to do is challenge those insecurities and question if they are really fair. Most of the time, they are not fair. When you're speaking to yourself, speak like you would with your best friend. For example, you wouldn't call your best friend worthless, so you shouldn't call yourself worthless either. It's okay to give yourself constructive criticism, but it is not okay to tear yourself down!

Forgive mistakes you have made. We all make mistakes. Mistakes are a normal part of life, and they help you grow. Many people think that if they had done something differently, they could have avoided their traumatic experience, but the truth is that trauma happens, it happens randomly. Yes, maybe certain decisions would have changed things, but lingering on those what if keeps you in the past and disenables you from looking towards the future. Use your mistakes to do better next time but know that bad things happen and mistakes are normal.

It's okay not to be perfect. Everyone has flaws, and being perfect would mean that you are not human. You won't always react in the best ways, and you won't always make the best choices, but none of that changes your value as a person. Being flawed does not inherently mean you are a bad person. Don't fall into the trap of all or nothing thinking. You're neither all good nor all bad. The world is a gradient place, and when you remember that, you can treat yourself with more compassion.

When you show yourself kindness, you're better able to show other people kindness as well. Kindness spreads. When you take the time to understand someone, you can better communicate with them, and the same applies to yourself. Your internal dialogue becomes more productive, and you start to understand your thinking better. You also learn to treat your loved ones with more kindness. Self-compassion teaches you to accept the flaws in life, and it allows you to let go of some of the crazy standards you hold for yourself. It shows you how to be more flexible and forgiving.

If you cannot be kind to yourself, it will be almost impossible for you to grow. Thus, you need to start talking to yourself with kinder language and finding things to love about yourself rather than things that you hate about yourself. You may not be able to love every part of yourself and your life, but you can love yourself overall and in spite of the things that you don't love.

Don't Forget to Include Your Loved Ones

More than just having loved ones around as a support system, you need to make your loved ones a part of your recovery process, and you need to help them with their struggles as well. Part of getting better is looking beyond yourself. You have to support your friends just as much as they support you. While recovery can often feel "me-centered," that's not really the case. It's about more than you. It's about your relationship with yourself and how that relationship impacts your relationship with the rest of the world. It means reconnecting because trauma can make you feel so distant from your own life.

Find people you can be honest about your struggles with, and don't let shame cause you to hide your trauma. You may be reticent to detail your hardships with people in your life. You might be afraid of burdening them. That feeling is pervasive in people who have mental health issues, and it can make you feel so alone. Be bold and share your experiences when appropriate. People who care about you will likely be glad to listen, and they'll want to know how you are doing. Don't share more than you are comfortable sharing, but do push yourself to share something. Even if you only share vague details, sharing creates stronger relationships.

Remember that boundaries are mutual. Your boundaries are important, but you also need to consider the boundaries that other people have. A hug, for example, could be comforting to you, but it could also trigger trauma that another person has. When another person has boundaries, you need to respect those boundaries and maintain that they respect yours as well. Any healthy relationship has boundaries, which detail what you each can offer and what lines you don't want to cross with that person. Boundaries will make you both feel safe as you support each other.

Be mindful that they may have a trauma as well. Unfortunately, trauma is all too common, so understand the ways in which people in your life may also struggle. Some people may want to help you, but they may be unable to exert that kind of energy because of their own struggles. It's hard to balance relationships when there is a lot of emotional baggage, but that effort makes sure that everyone feels comfortable and that the relationship is balanced. If you don't consider the trauma other people may have, you may take support from the other person without adequately giving it back.

Always appreciate your friends' efforts. Show that you are grateful to have supportive people in your life. Friends need to feel appreciated and to be reassured about their roles in your life. While it's normal for friends to support one another, you should still show that you are glad to have them in your life. This gratitude can come in a number of ways, but you should be aware that some people will feel appreciated when you say, "Thank you for listening," while others may prefer that you show your gratitude with a hug or other gestures. Get to know what makes people in your life feel appreciated and use those methods to communicate your gratitude with them. Show gratitude regularly.

Not all relationships are worth keeping. It is sad to lose relationships, but not all relationships are meant to last forever. Some people do you more harm than good, and even if you care about those people, you may have to cut them out of your life for your mental health. Even if you can't or don't want to cut them out entirely, thinking about the role they play in your life may help. Relationships change over time, and when you need to, you should renegotiate boundaries. Monitor how well your relationships are functioning and adjust accordingly. Be upfront about concerns you have; the other person has no obligation to change based on your feedback, but it can be nice to give them the opportunity before cutting them out of your life.

This book has made the value of relationships abundantly clear, but relationships can never be one-sided. You have to support the people in your life. While support should never be transactional, it is the basis for strong relationships. Remember that you do not exist within a bubble, and by keeping that in mind, you will ensure that your relationships endure and help you more than they hurt you.

Open Yourself to Change

You need to open your mind to change. Many people shut down the idea of changing before they have even tried it. Not much happens when you refuse to change, though. Sometimes, things even get worse. Refusing to change often causes restlessness, and it makes you feel like your life is going nowhere. Even if you're doing things well, if you don't have hope for anything better, you feel stuck. Humans strive to be more than we are now, which means that you need to break down the barriers that are making you hesitant to change. Of course, this task is not as easy as it sounds, but by diving into change, you can transform your life.

Each morning, you should tell yourself, "I am committed to change." You might not mean it at first, but as time ticks on, you will get used to the idea. This affirmation reminds you of your openness, and it gets your subconscious brain to listen to what you want it to do. Your brain may take some convincing, but if you repeat this mantra each day, it will start to get the message. Commit yourself to change because once you commit, it is harder to back down. Share this commitment with a friend, or write it down in your journal to hold yourself even more accountable!

Remember that when you refuse to change, you cannot go anywhere. You're in a perpetual state of flux. Maybe you aren't the worst, but you can never be your best when you refuse to take chances and confront the dark areas of your brain. You need to will yourself towards the scary unknown. If you don't, you will always be living in the past, wondering how things could be rather than taking charge and making things how you want them to be. Don't be a passive bystander in your life. Take control right now, and accept change.

Imagine what you would most like to do that trauma prevents you from doing. Trauma often feels like a jail. It makes it impossible for you to enjoy or even attempt some of the things that should give you happiness. It can make you feel depressed and scared, so remind yourself that change will allow you to get out of the trap you are in. Change is the only way to overcome your trauma, so by thinking about what you have to lose when you stay the same, you put things into perspective. Loss is a lot more potent than gain.

Know that change doesn't always bring happiness, and that's okay. Sometimes, the changes you make will slap you in the face. They'll go in a direction that you didn't predict, and they'll make you doubt yourself and your future. Not all change is good, but it is necessary. Unexpected things happen whether you want them to or not, so no matter how much you try to maintain the status quo, something will change eventually. At least when you make the conscious effort to promote change, you have some role in determining what happens to you. Things can still get messed up, but not for lack of trying! Some changes will hurt, but keep pushing to find change that makes you feel good.

Never forget that the greatest things in life come after discomfort. When you are uncomfortable, you are learning. If you go through life doing what is comfortable, you never push your boundaries. You stagnate. Think of great inventors. Thomas Edison failed to make the lightbulb hundreds of times, but he kept trying, even though his investment could have led to more disappointment. Revolutionary people take risks. They try to create change, even if that change may turn sour as it unfolds. You're going to feel out of your element sometimes, but that means you're tantalizingly close to something magnificent.

Think of mistakes as chances to do better next time. Mistakes don't mean you're a bad person. People often get stuck in the mindset that making a mistake means there is something wrong with them. Mistakes help you learn. Babies learn to walk by falling down! No kid just suddenly walks without issue. They keep trying. They fall, and then, they stand up. They change the way they move, and that change allows them to then run and play and do more. New endeavors take time to figure out, and it's the mistakes that point you towards the finish line; they show you what you need to do differently.

Focus on what you can control rather than what you cannot control. There is so much in life that you have no power over. Don't worry so much about those things because, at the end of the day, they'll happen whether you permit them to or not. Bad things happen in life that you have no power over, but you do have power over the good actions you choose to do. If the rainstorm comes, the rainstorm comes, but you have the choice to look at the radar and pack your raingear. You can make the best of the rain rather than worrying about when the rain will happen and hoping to prevent it.

Try new things! One of the best ways to promote change is to try new things. Push your boundaries and set goals about what you would like to try. If there's something that you've been considering doing, do it! Don't keep putting off activities that would give you happiness because you are afraid of the unknowns that come with change. Try a sport that fascinates you, or go on an adventure. It doesn't matter what you do differently, but you should do something differently. Even just changing the way you drive to work can challenge the mindset that keeps you stuck, so if you have to, start small and build your way up to do other new things.

Change makes you a better person, and it allows the growth that you want. Change is intimidating. It makes you wonder if you're on the wrong course. Sometimes, it fails, but it will enliven you. It liberates you and guides you towards the things that will help you combat your trauma and create a growth mindset.

Your Trauma Can Make You Better

As you continue your journey, remember these details so that you can maintain your progress. Never forget the ways your trauma can make you better because as much as trauma represents the worst part of your life, it also signifies the chance to be strong and brave.

As much as trauma hurts, it's also a chance to do something differently. It's an opportunity to take the darkness and turn it into something productive. Destruction means that there's plenty of room for construction, so while it won't be easy, you can be better as a result of the way your trauma has shaped you. Trauma changes you, and it can make you stronger. The post-traumatic growth encouraged in this book proves that such is the case. Throughout this book, you have learned to not just be resilient but to be better than ever, and now's the time to make those changes. Life isn't going to wait, so it's time to make the necessary changes right now.

When you hurt, you have so much room to grow because pain is human. You have been through a lot. You've felt pain, and you have worried about your wellbeing. This worry is pressing, and it can make you reluctant to try anything to better yourself. Trauma lingers, and it is your brain's way of protecting you and keeping you safe from the potential perils of life. There's a reason for trauma, and so it's nothing to be ashamed of. It's a normal part of humanity, and when you have PTSD, your symptoms are severe, but they are human. Your humanity allows you to make the most of the hardships you endure.

Your trauma allows you to relate better to others. Your trauma can be a connective force. It shows you how to be sympathetic and compassionate. Without trauma of your own, it may be hard to understand other people's suffering. Your trauma can motivate you to be kinder to others and treat them in a way that allows them to heal and grow as well. Humans thrive when we connect, so trauma can facilitate that connection like nothing else. Shared experiences bring us together, and they remind us that for all our differences, we still share so much. Don't be afraid of this connection because it can enrich your life, and when you learn you're not alone, you unlock the new potential that is inherent when you look beyond yourself.

Trauma can also help you understand yourself. When you hurt, you have to look inward. You have to learn to analyze your feelings and process them. Trauma doesn't happen in a vacuum. It is often motivated by outside forces, insecurities, and fears. When you have to confront your trauma, you may have to confront other parts of yourself that you never paid attention to before. There are lots of ways of getting to know yourself, but when you have trauma, you have the opportunity to reach into the ugly parts of yourself until you find slivers of beauty. Trauma makes you more aware, and you can use that awareness to figure out what you really want from life.

People who overcome their trauma learn resilience in all areas of your life. You learn coping skills and how to problem solve through your trauma. While post-traumatic growth prides itself on reaching beyond resilience, resilience is still important. It allows you to bounce back from things that hurt you or stop you from reaching your goals. You can always go beyond resilience, of course, but if you can't be resilient, you can't go forward either. In moments when you don't know how to grow, at the very least, you need to be resilient, or your trauma will eat you up inside and slowly destroy your well being. Resilient people know how to take the first steps towards growth.

While trauma can highlight the horrors of the world, it can also magnify the good. When you have been hurt, surely there were people who responded with kindness. For instance, imagine that you were in a traumatic car accident. Maybe a bystander helped save your life on that day. The accident was awful, but the way people reached out to you and tried to help you hopefully wasn't that awful. Think of all the good people and forces that surrounded you as you dealt with your trauma. When a loved one dies, people often send over casseroles and flowers to boost your spirits, and while those behaviors don't take away the loss, they remind you that good still exists in the world and that awfulness cannot erase that good.

Remember that you are more than your trauma, but your trauma is no doubt a part of who you are and who you will be, but you get to decide how you let that trauma impact you. When you make a choice to challenge your mindset and employ a toolbox of coping tools, you start to build a brighter future that can be whatever you want it to be. Your future can be the brightest part of your life. Trauma doesn't mean that your best years are past, and it doesn't mean that you're an entirely new person. Trauma is pain, and that pain can manifest in a number of ways. You can learn to mediate this pain.

Trauma doesn't have to be the end of your life! Traumatic events feel like the end of the world, and when you develop traumatic disorders, you feel out of control over the influence of that trauma. Yet, there are things you can control, and PTSD is treatable. It doesn't have to make you feel like a shell of yourself. You can grow from your trauma using the techniques that were outlined in this book. I know that it may seem like an uphill battle, but it's a normal course of healing. You don't have to live with open wounds forever, nor should you. Trauma has long motivated people to do better and be better. Through our mistakes and mishaps, we become stronger, and we are so much more than resilient. We grow, and we thrive, and we tell our trauma that we are stronger than it. You are stronger than your PTSD or trauma, and it takes time to get better, but you can take steps to recovery right now.

CONCLUSION

Y ou have completed *Post-Traumatic Growth Mindset: The Complete Guidebook of Techniques of PTSD Healing and Recovery*, and I hope it was an enlightening experience for you. This book should propel you towards your goals and give you the chance you need to make the progress you deserve. You've made significant progress in your growth simply by reading this book. You have learned some mechanisms you can use to overcome your trauma and piece your life back together. Trauma has a devastating impact on so many people, but your trauma doesn't have to define you. Like so many other people have learned, you can defy your trauma and use that trauma to be better in the end. It's scary to confront that trauma, but it is not impossible.

You deserve to have the future that you want. Whatever guilt or doubt that plagues you, you deserve a brighter future. You have inherent value, and I want you to dig deep in yourself and embrace that value. You are not a lost cause, and the trauma you experienced was not your fault. Trauma is something that is out of our control, but our response to trauma is within our power. Take back control of your life.

The next step is to follow up on the lessons you have learned and apply them to your life. Don't let the chance pass you by. It's time to dive into this process. Now that you have this information, there's no reason why you shouldn't use it. Whatever worries you have about this process, put them aside for just a little while. Try these techniques full-heartedly, even if you're skeptical.

Don't waste time letting your trauma continue to haunt you. Many people like to put self-development off. They insist that they can address their issues tomorrow, but there is always another tomorrow, so you should embrace your future right now. Don't wait to make changes. You cannot change everything that is wrong in one day, but you can start making changes right now. It will be easier to keep going once you have some momentum. You can't guarantee that things will get better unless you take the steps necessary to make them better! Don't keep waiting for your trauma to heal on its own! Your time is precious, so start using it in ways that provide more joy and less pain.

You cannot change your past, but you can define your future. Never forget that you have autonomy. As much as it may seem that your trauma controls you, you're the one that controls it. You feed into your mindset, and while you cannot control everything your mind does, you can influence how your brain functions. You're not doomed to live with your harmful state of mind forever, and as soon as you remember that, you will see profound differences in your everyday decision-making and how you feel.

Please remember that this book is not a substitution for medical advice. While some people can overcome their PTSD without outside resources, it's important to discuss your concerns with your doctor or a mental health professional if you are struggling. These professionals can guide you and ensure that you are getting the level of care that you need to thrive and grow as a person. The tips in this book are effective but remain mindful of how you are feeling and seek help if you ever need it. There's nothing shameful about reaching out to a professional. Learning when to ask for help is one of the most beneficial lessons you can learn in life! No one is an expert in everything, after all.

Please leave a review on this book if it was helpful to you! It would also be great if you shared this book with a loved one. Whether that loved one has PTSD or not, this book gives them insight, and it can help them improve their relationship with trauma, but it can also give them the tools and knowledge that they need to better help you. With all that in mind, thank you yet again for reading, and now it's time for you to go out in the world and embrace all that life has to offer. You're on your way towards amazing things!

www.ingramcontent.com/pod-product-compliance
Lightning Source LLC
Chambersburg PA
CBHW070932030426
42336CB00014BA/2638